Towards a Unified Theory of Mind: Psychoanalysis as Art and Science

LAWRENCE DUGAN, Ph.D.

Strategic Book Publishing

Strategic Book Publishing
An imprint of Strategic Book Group
P. O. Box 333
Durham, CT 06422
www.StrategicBookGroup.com

ISBN: 978-1-60911-295-0

Printed in the United States of America

Book Design: Judy Maenle

To all who love God and
to all who love learning
I dedicate this book.

Acknowledgements

Deep thanks to the following:

Almighty God for giving me the intellect to absorb knowledge and the passion to share it.

Margaret, my wife, who has shared laughter and endured challenges with me these many years.

My mother and father for guiding and molding me while letting me be me.

My children and grandchildren, who just give me love.

All the great teachers who have inspired me.

My friends Mike Demorest and Gary Mederven and all my friends at Cascade Christian Church.

Mrs. Calabash and all those who—however unwittingly—bring joy to my soul.

Almighty God, Who put all these people into my life.

Contents

Preface

The concepts underlying this book have been percolating in my mind and heart for years. Psychoanalyzing myself revealed the exceptional ambivalence permeating my soul—an ambivalence that precluded me from acting on my desire to write, including questioning my ability to write anything worthwhile.

Then, on February 6, 2009—near midnight—I had a heart attack. That experience propelled me into changing my life in many ways—not the least of which was to compel myself to complete this manuscript.

Over the course of the past forty-one years, I have conducted psychological and neuropsychological evaluations on more than four thousand individuals, provided psychoanalytic psychotherapy to hundreds of persons, studied research findings from a half dozen different disciplines, served as a business consultant to a dozen companies and worked with physicians in treating psychosomatic symptoms using hypnoanalysis/hypnotherapy. During that time patients and students have asked me dozens of questions, some common and some not so common: Does hypnosis work? How does hypnosis work? Can positive thinking prevent cancer? Why do I feel like hitting people when I hear someone use the word *create*? Why do serial killers become serial killers? Does anyone ever get over being abused as a child? Why do women stay in abusive relationships? Why do some people succeed and others not?

Not content with merely answering individual questions, I challenged myself to create a framework that integrated the answers to these questions with research findings, clinical experience, observations of society and the thinking of scientists

1

who have preceded me. I do not stand alone is this regard. Dr. V. J. Ramachandran, who has been identified as one of the one hundred most important scientists to watch in the twenty-first century, reports that as he gives talks around the country, the one question people ask again and again is: "When are brain scientists going to come up with a unified theory for how the brain works? Physics has Einstein's general theory of relativity and Newton's universal law of gravitation. Why not one for the brain?" Change the word "brain" to "mind," and what I set out to formulate will become clear.

Towards a Unified Theory of Mind: Psychoanalysis as Art and Science represents the result of my efforts. I am, and always have been, driven by a perverse need **to** unify diverse elements and/or theories that may seem to be completely unrelated to one another. This habit has remained with me since childhood and reflects the fact that underlying this book are certain often unstated beliefs. The first belief maintains that with a perspective broad enough science will discover parallelism in all dimensions of the universe. As stated below, the development of the fetus parallels the development of the brain, which—in turn—provides a template for viewing the development of the human personality.

The second belief focuses on the human tendency to overlook similarities and focus on unimportant differences. This parallels the metaphor of the six blind men and the elephant, none of whom sees—or seeks—the entirety of the subject. Aligned with this tendency has been the tendency of many to deify a position so as to exclude continued investigation and questioning.

A third belief asserts that working with the human mind means committing to endless questioning and study and striving constantly to absorb new findings and modify whatever theories we hold in the cause of Truth. It also means looking far beyond traditional boundaries to see what is there.

These beliefs set the stage for this book, which starts by presenting a brief history of psychoanalysis—arguably among the most significant breakthroughs in thinking over the past 110 years. Following that history comes a simplified review of fetal development and brain development, setting the stage for understanding a proposed unified theory of personality. The closing chapters examine the future of psychoanalysis, focusing on the science (process) involved and the art (skill of the analyst) required.

A brief history of psychoanalysis

Two hundred years ago Alexander Pope wrote: "A little learning is a dangerous thing; drink deep, or taste not the Pierian spring." While this warning readily applies to any field of study, it stands as particularly imperative in the enterprise known as Psychoanalysis—the art and science of striving to understand the human mind, heart and soul. To understand this Science of Understanding, as it were, requires reviewing—however briefly—the core of the history of psychoanalysis.

Psychoanalysis—like every other science—has evolved significantly over the course of the past one hundred years. Beginning in 1895, with Freud's unifying diverse observations and strands of thinking regarding hysterical disorders, psychoanalysis evolved, in a nonlinear fashion, into multidimensional aggregate thinking about mankind and mental disorders. For forty-four years Freud and his followers studied unconscious mental processes and their role in narcissism (1915), depression (1917) and self-destructive behavior and masochism (1919).

Together with his followers Freud elaborated an entire theory of mental functioning, clarified intrapsychic conflict as the cause of anxiety and delineated how anxiety could impact intellectual functioning including speech and thinking. By 1936 Robert Waelder, a disciple of Freud, clarified the "Principle of Multiple Function" widening the formulation that psychological symptoms were both caused by and relieved conflict simultaneously. Also in 1936, Anna Freud, Sigmund's daughter, published her seminal book, *The Ego and the Mechanisms of Defense*, which established the numerous ways the mind could shut upsetting things out of consciousness.

Though Freud ostensibly claimed that psychoanalysis as a scientific system remained open to revision as new facts and observations accumulated, his behavior did not seem to reflect that belief. When, in 1926, Otto Rank—for twenty years Freud's "chosen one"—postulated that there were pre-Oedipal sources of anxiety, Freud denounced and ostracized him. The remainder of Freud's disciples, the most influential analysts of the time, joined with Freud in condemning Rank.

Rank's defection from the orthodoxy of psychoanalysis, though the first, soon became the first of many. Freud's death in 1939 left psychoanalysis without the unifying leadership he had intended and opened the door to a number of new theories to the point where today there exist at least twenty-two different theoretical orientations labeling themselves as psychoanalytic. This rainbow spectrum of theoretical orientations creates problems in striving to address issues concerning psychoanalysis.

Freud's death also triggered in American society an upsurge in interest in psychoanalytic thinking leading to a proliferation of psychoanalytic writings that may have reached its zenith in 1954 with the publication of *The Fifty Minute Hour* by Dr. Robert Lindner. At almost precisely that same time, radically new thinking regarding a psychoanalytic perspective on normal development emerged in the work of Erikson's psychosocial theory (*Childhood and Society,* 1950). Though Erikson's early influence limited itself to academia, within thirty years Eriksonian approaches became increasingly in evidence as a treatment modality.

Psychoanalysis sustained a high degree of visibility through the 1960's and 70's as movie stars and other notables underwent treatment. Psychological concepts became popularized in films and plays. New dimensions of psychoanalysis emerged. Books including psychological themes—such as *Scruples* and *Mistral's Daughter* by Judy Krantz and *Looking for Mr. Goodbar* by Judith Rossner became best sellers. In 1983, Judith Rossner's work *August* became the first popularized account of an analysis focusing on pre-Oedipal issues.

Starting in the 1980's the popularity of psychoanalysis declined steadily. In the sciences by the late 70's and early 80's medical schools became more dependent on grants from pharmaceutical companies, leading to chairs of psychiatry departments in the nation's medical schools to emerge from backgrounds involving pharmacological research rather than from analytic training. Circa 1986 insurance companies decimated health insurance coverage for psychoanalytic treatment, based on the fact that long-term psychoanalytic treatment had become too costly and new medications were available to treat a wide variety of disorders.

However, not all the decline in medical psychoanalysis occurred as a result of external factors. The fractionalization of psychoanalysis into different schools representing Topographic, Dynamic (conflict oriented), Economic, Structural and Ego Psychology (an adaptational perspective) created confusion for the scientific community and general society. Psychoanalysis itself lost a coherent identity. As a result Freud's more devoted followers felt they needed to be constantly in the position of having to defend Freud's views—and institutionalize them. Freud's system then became, in the hands of some of his followers and defenders, orthodoxy—a dogma upon which all theoretical innovation, clinical observation and therapeutic practice had to be grounded. Elkind comments that surrendering progress to maintain loyalty to Freud's authority rather than observing and deciding on the basis of data what is true and what is false has contributed to the disrepute in which psychoanalysis is widely held today.

The fractionalizing of psychoanalytic theory has led to therapists, medical professionals and society in general to lose sight of the common underpinnings shared by ventures labeled psychoanalytic despite differences in practice and theoretical orientations. This book represents an effort to clarify the underpinnings of psychoanalytic practice and embed those in the context of a theory that will embrace current—and future—observations and knowledge. In so doing, certain basic premises are set forth:

Psychoanalysis for our purposes is best identified as the process of two persons, one with comprehensive specialized knowledge about human beings, interacting in a free and unstructured manner for the benefit of the one of them identified as patient. The very nature of that description demands that psychoanalysis be viewed as both art and science. As manifest in *The Fifty Minute Hour*, psychoanalysis evolves from the person of the therapist-analyst. In his foreword, Lindner writes, ".it is the self of the analyst that is the common element in all of the tales." There is no formula, just as there is no formula for a dancer interpreting a given piece of music. Once there is a mandate that every step be just so, the dance loses the essence of dance and becomes a parody of freedom. The same stands true for psychoanalysis. One crucial implication of this observation lies in the dilemma it can create for replicability of treatment results.

Psychoanalysis encompasses both knowledge and belief: *"For those who believe, no proof* is necessary. *For those* who disbelieve, *no* amount of *proof is sufficient."* St. Ignatius of Loyola.

I write for the intelligent lay reader while hoping and trusting that those with psychoanalytic sophistication will find new prods to their own thinking. I use case histories, examples and metaphors to give each reader a springboard to his/her own experiences and, hopefully, deeper understanding and appreciation of the material.

Erikson's psychosocial theory serves as the best framework within which to examine psychoanalysis—and particularly the future direction of psychoanalysis. As delineated here, Eriksonian Theory operates within a realm of development emphasizing inner conflicts predicated on external interactions. Throughout the analysis of Eriksonian stages, the material alludes to integrating Erikson's theory with more traditional psychoanalytic concepts—viewing the two theoretical frameworks as representing the intrapsychic and extrapsychic elements of a common theory.

The version of Erikson's theory presented here has been modified—based on clinical experience and review of research—from Erikson's original conceptualization where he postulated two choices for each stage of development to suggesting that each stage actually presents the individual with three options or pathways to resolve the developmental conflict.

"Psychoanalytic" as used here signifies the most basic concepts in psychoanalytic thinking, i.e., the uncovering of unconscious thoughts, feelings and conflicts that direct human behavior without a person's awareness, that uncovering being necessary to changing behavior, thoughts and feelings.

Understanding the development of the human mind and personality starts with the premise that mental development parallels biological development. Therefore, Chapter One serves to focus on basic concepts by giving an overview of fetal development from a single-celled entity to the multibillion cell multisystemic organism we become at birth—including the development of the physical structure underlying our mind and personality, the brain. Chapter Two details the early stages of our mental-emotional-social development. Chapter Three gives an overview of Eriksonian theory. Chapters Four through Eleven elaborate on each developmental stage and attendant conflicts.

Chapter Twelve analyzes and critiques narrow-band psychoanalytic thinking. Chapter Thirteen focuses on the science of psychoanalysis (the "process"), while Chapter Fourteen addresses the art of psychoanalysis (i.e., the person of the analyst). Chapter Fifteen offers closing thoughts on the future of psychoanalysis.

CHAPTER 1

Basic Development

"Ontogeny recapitulates phylogeny" has become a catch phrase familiar to virtually any student who studies biological sciences. One understands that as an advanced organism develops, it will pass through stages that resemble the adult phase of less advanced organism. Such thinking suggests that in our universe there exists a parallelism—however ethereal—that only needs to be discovered in order to be understood.

In pursuing an understanding of our mental development, therefore, we can postulate that psychic or mental development will parallel in some manner the physical development of our bodies and brains from conception to birth. Analyzing the fundamentals of human growth gives us a model to extend to all human development.

Physical Development

After the egg and sperm connect to form the single-celled zygote, the zygote travels down the fallopian tube towards the uterus—doubling from one cell to two, then four, then eight, etc, as it goes. Seven days after conception, one sperm and one egg have become several hundred cells, resembling a very small raspberry. At this juncture, we label the entity a blastocyst.

The blastocyst has not yet burrowed into the uterine lining—it moves slowly down the fallopian tube preparing to implant. While it is doing so, though, the cells divide into two groups. The inner group of cells will develop into the embryo. The outer group of cells will become the membranes that nourish and protect the embryo.

Specialization has begun. At about thirteen days following conception, the blastocyst implants itself in the wall of mother's uterus, and the placenta—the organ connecting baby to mother —develops. This connecting allows the embryo (the new name of the blastocyst to receive nourishment from the mother and expel wastes for the mom to eliminate with her own.

In week three of fetal development, cells start to specialize. Various cells migrate to different corners to receive instructions to become types and to create separate organs and body parts such as a skeleton, the digestive system, the circulatory system, or a brain. Before the end of three weeks, a rudimentary nervous system begins to form. This neural center will supervise the rapid fetal development to follow.

By day twenty-one, the embryo has a rudimentary spinal column, brain and heart. The cells that will become eyes appear as disks on top of the "head." Ear cells are present and waiting to activate. This tiny, three week old collection of cells has a vascular system that pumps gently around the body; it has, in essence, a heartbeat and a delivery system for blood and oxygen. From conception to this stage requires three weeks; the embryo has developed from one cell into millions and is visible to the naked eye. More importantly, cells of different types have emerged to create organs with specialized functions.

Development of the Human Brain

By day twenty-one, the embryo has three different types of tissue: the ectoderm which includes all of the packaging elements of the organism, i.e., skin, hair, nails and, interestingly enough, the nervous system; the mesoderm that makes up the major structural components of the body, including the great muscle masses—both voluntary and involuntary; and the endoderm that includes all of the cell systems that constitute our organs and vessels and make up the lining for those organs.

Once the basic process of creating three types of cells has been completed, cells from the mesoderm—in a process six hundred million years old—forms a long cylindrical structure. This rod like structure is the notochord, the progenitor of the backbone or vertebral column. As the embryo continues developing, the notochord has a highly specific "organizing influence" on the primitive ectoderm layer just above it. Through the release of special chemicals, the overlying ectoderm is induced to divide more rapidly, forming a thickened mass called the neural plate. A crease or fold soon appears in this plate. The crease rapidly deepens and becomes known as the neural groove. The entire embryo is lengthening as this happens. The neural groove continues to deepen until its sides, the neural folds, arch over and fuse with each other forming a short segment of completely enclosed tube. This newly formed "neural tube" will become the nervous system. This leads to the brain developing five vesicles that become the five major subdivisions of the brain: cerebral hemispheres, diencephalon, midbrain, pons and cerebellum and medulla oblongata.

Now the single layer of primitive ectoderm divides very rapidly and will, in time, form virtually all of the central nervous system (brain and spinal cord). Specialization continues and different types of cells are created to form the peripheral nerves, roots and ganglion cells of the peripheral nervous system

Cell division continues at an exponential pace (doubling every ninety minutes). After a period of active replication, some of these primitive daughter cells initiate the next step in brain development, leaving the home base (the multiplication zone) and moving to the outer edges. The most dramatic thickening of the original neural tube occurs in the area of the developing cerebral hemispheres.

The cerebral cortex of higher forms is made up of six cell layers. Each layer has its distinct pattern of organization and connections. Initially, the cells move in to form the deepest or sixth (closest to the center of the brain) layer. The fifth layer covers that first layer; subsequent layers coat the layer that preceded them. Once the primitive migrating nerve cells have reached their final position, they begin to develop extensions from their cell bodies. These will progressively become longer and form the two major types of processes or branches, which characterize almost all neurons, dendrites and the axon.

The second major type of cell extension, the axon, also sets out to establish connections with many other neurons—both near and far away. Imagine how far an axon must migrate from the cortex if its target area is the lower spinal cord of a basketball player!

The elaborate structure (architecture) of the brain thus involves ensembles of neurons, their dendritic branches and their projective axons that communicate via a myriad of connections known as synapses. Each synapse is a point of contiguity (but not necessarily continuity) between two neural elements. In the vast majority of these synapses, small amounts of chemicals (neurotransmitters) are released, crossing the infinitesimal gap between the two elements, thereby carrying the neural message to the next element. Tens of thousands of synapses may cover the dendrites and cell body surface of a single neuron, leading to the statement: "There are more possible interconnections in the human brain than there are atoms in the universe." However true that may be, by estimate there are trillions of synapses in your brain. There may be as many as one hundred neurotransmitters and neuromodulators associated with these synapses further multiplying the vast range of possible interaction patterns at these junctions.

One curious mechanism in cortical development has to do with the stratagem of developing temporary connections. Neurons will connect with one another via dendrite or axon until more definitive (and more functional?) connections takes place. Scientists investigating this phenomenon speculate that a number of major and minor cognitive and emotional disorders, which will show up at various stages in the life of the individual, result from temporary connections that were not temporary—though they were intended to be.

Synapse formation probably starts in the mid or late second trimester and continues during the life of the individual. Careful ultramicroscopic studies show that synapse formation proceeds at its highest rate during the first six to eight years of postnatal life, a period of enormous information input and acquisition— social, environmental, linguistic, etc. The growing brain may well be in its most sponge like phase of learning as the child becomes acquainted with the endless range of symbols, rules, facts and behaviors that make it a member of its culture.

Structure of the Human Brain

The adult human brain consists of three different but interconnected brains: our reptilian brain, our mammalian brain and our cerebral cortex. The manner in which these three brains interact with each other underlies human behavior.

Reptilian Brain

The ancient most primitive part of our brain is the innermost core reptilian brain. This portion of the brain appears largely unchanged by evolution, and we share it with all other animals that have a backbone. This reptilian brain controls body functions required for sustaining life such as breathing and body temperature. At this level of evolution—the human level—behavior relating to survival of the species, such as sexual behavior, is directed by the reptilian brain, and is instinctive. Responses are automatic. Territory is acquired by force and defended. Might is right.

The reptilian brain lacks sophistication. It engages in a type of thinking best referred to as "black-white thinking," "kill or be killed," and "fight or flee." The relevance of this for forming first images and introjects (object relations theory) will be delineated below.

Mammalian Brain

Next to evolve from the reptilian brain is the mammalian brain, adding new functions and new ways of controlling the body including automatic control of body functions such as digestion, the fluid balance, body temperature and blood pressure (autonomic nervous system, hypothalamus). The mammalian brain includes specialized cells for filing new experiences as they happen and so creating a store of experience based memories (hippocampus). With this development, the brain creates the capacity for experience based recognition of danger and for responding to this according to past experience.

The mammalian brain contributes the capacity for its possessor to have conscious feelings about events (amygdala). Thus, the mammal has greater consciousness of itself in relation to the environment. Millions of neural pathways connect the hippocampal and amygdala structures to the reptilian brain leading to behavior being less rigidly controlled by instincts and to a decrease in black-white thinking. Feelings such as attachment, anger and fear (with attendant behavioral response patterns of care, fight or flight) emerge. With the addition of the mammalian brain, new and distinctive patterns of organization have been added to the behavioral repertoire.

Neocortex (also referred to as "hominid" or "human" brain)

Then evolves the third part of the brain, the neocortex (the grey matter), the bulk of the brain in two symmetrical hemispheres, separated but communicating (by another specially designed set of brain structures). And this third brain transforms mere mammal into human by the massive grey matter (neocortex—which envelopes most of the earlier brain and amounts to about eighty-five percent of the human brain mass), as well as attendant totally different layers and levels of organization and new abilities.

The two hemispheres, which are covered by an outer layer and interconnected by a string of nerve fibers, are separated by a groove. The fibers that connect the two lie at the base of the groove. With the mammalian brain emerged feelings such as attachment, fear and anger and associated behavioral response patterns. With the neocortex came far more complex emotions and connections, with those advanced human emotional responses dependent on neuronal pathways linking the right hemisphere to the mammalian brain, which in turn is linked by other pathways to the even older reptilian brain.

Work is divided between the two halves of the brain, each with its different functions, though they supplement and cooperate with each other. A simple summary of the functional division of activities between the two hemispheres would be:

Left Hemisphere	Right Hemisphere
Communicates by using words	Communicates using pictures
Has highly developed verbal abilities	Has highly developed spatial abilities
Is logical and systematic	Is intuitive and imaginative—and emotional
Concerns itself with matters as they are	Concerns itself with what can be
Responsible for word choice and meaning	Responsible for emotional content of speech

It is the right hemisphere that links to the primitive older part of the brain, communicating using images with its primitive 'unconscious' functions. Thinking in pictures is fast. Think of how long it takes to describe a picture, a scene, in words and compare this with the speed of taking it in by looking at it. But images may be described, or transformed into a narrative, by the left hemisphere.

So the now human brain includes the processing and memorizing of images and of their components and assigning both meaning and emotion to those images. Language develops and with it corresponding mental processing connected with memory and memorizing—joined with the development of a wide range of emotions, of feelings, of care and affection, and the capability for transforming those into action. Add in objective and logical thinking and evaluation and the capacity for imagining, and the human brain now constitutes the perfect structure within which the human mind and personality can develop and the perfect tool to make that development happen.

CHAPTER 2

Development of the Human Mind

By three weeks of age, the reptilian brain functions have established themselves and work to preserve the life of the embryo, pumping blood, breathing, etc. This very act creates in the higher mammalian brain some form of consciousness and feeling. In the womb, the embryo experiences this primal awareness as a feeling best translated as, "I am the world" accompanied by an undefined fantasy of omnipotence. Even in the protected environment, the developing fetus can experience and respond to stimuli. In the same manner as cells divided as the original zygote grew, each experience divides or splits off to become an entity unto itself. At some point, the accumulation of experiences leads the mind to move from, "I am the world" to the premise, "I am and the world is," establishing that the two are separate, mirroring the original split of the zygote and other divisions (splitting of the types of cells from one into three, the neural matter from one to two). This process represents the first step in the hierarchical organization of the mind—paralleling what happens in neurological development, the notochord having an organizing effect on the ectoderm. This dichotomy may best represent the baby's mental status up until the time birth occurs—while individual mental-experiential units accrue and perhaps become organized into a hierarchy or categorical system.

With birth, the world of the infant changes significantly. From an environment with controlled stimuli and relatively constant temperature, the brain becomes flooded with thousands of sensations impinging on it simultaneously. One result of this flooding involves the brain's developing temporary connections in striving to cope with this flood. From what we know of the sets of interconnections in the brain, the raw data coming in will be taken in by the neocortex (or hominid brain) and sent down through the mammalian brain, where specialized cells will identify new experiences and compare them to old one while creating feelings associated with that experience, to the reptilian brain, where primal (black-white) emotional responses are generated (terror, fight, flight, etc.)

Gradually—with the accumulation of thousands of experiences and sensory data, the infant constructs a degree of consciousness about itself in relation to the environment. Simultaneously, it constructs both memories and fantasies of the environment and memories and fantasies of self and others—providing the foundation for having hundreds, if not thousands, of internalized images of "objects"—people and sounds and feelings—all of which will need to eventually be united. Just as the blastocyst at a certain stage of development resembled a small raspberry, the images the infant creates of "self'" and "the other" can be imagined as small (psychic) raspberries with dozens or more of self-representations waiting to be unified by additional experiences and the upper levels of the cortex as it processes information. To add to the complexity, each image has attached to it via dendritic connections any number of emotions from both the reptilian brain and the mammalian brain.

Synapses form at an exponential rate, flooding the brain with incalculable information about the world, others, self, feelings and imaginings—all lying in what later we identify as the unconscious since the hominid mind (cortex) has not yet developed the integrated reflectiveness required for analyzing.

With experience, discrete units of memory (with their attendant feelings) combine to form images. The image of "mother," for example, can include the "good breast," the "bad breast," warmth, distance, soothing voice, different touches and thousands of events and sensations impossible to imagine.

With repeated constant experience the infant will form a smaller number of images—some of which may still conflict with one another—that lead him to feel safe and cared for—even if by different mothering figures. If the "mothering" is inconsistent or consistently cold or consistently painful, the infant will create an image of the world that defies our ability to define or understand—an image that will bring with it terror, rage, helplessness, self-loathing and more. The image of "self" created will be that of worthlessness, revenge-seeking and death-seeking.

Even when the infant's overall experience is "only good enough," the potential is high for significant early experiences to impact an infant's conceptualizations to such a degree that they carry forward and dictate irrational adult behavior and feelings. A mother's illness, a mother losing her own parent or a mother returning to work and leaving the infant in the care of an inadequate care-giver, for example, will create distortions in the infant's constructions and fantasies—distortions that will endure into adulthood impacting behavior, thoughts and feelings. The case of Matt V (See Chapter 13) represents one example of this phenomenon.

In situations where the infant finds no primary figure to attach to, depression and despair will constitute the more likely outcomes. When a primary care-giver has been there and is then removed, the infant will feel deprived, rage-filled and vengeful. In both instances, the black-white thinking of the reptilian brain will dominate elements in the mammalian brain and, at times, disrupt patterns of organization based on survival needs—as reflected in Bar-Levav's premises about an infant's fear of annihilation, abandonment and absorption.

Throughout this process the infant's emotions organize and focus every experience. With every change in the environment, with every movement a baby makes, sensations continue to accrue to become embedded in a network of memories and comparisons. Hierarchies are built and then abandoned or modified in an ever-learning, acquisitive mode of all three brains. The need for more space to store all this information leads to the cerebral cortex increasing the storage space available by folding in on itself, i.e., pushing down surface area to develop crevices and fissures—thus increasing area available for storage and ease of communication among different parts of the brain.

As more and more information is exchanged among the three brains, several events occur simultaneously. First, the infant has—and shows—an ever-increasing consciousness as reflected in orientation and attention, responsivity, deliberate movements and moods. The content of consciousness at any given moment consists of the brain's awareness of only a small fraction of what is proceeding on the inside (inside the unconscious).

Second, the development of unconscious connections continues. Since these connections are subcortical (prelanguage), they will reside in the unconscious and can continue to dominate behavior for a lifetime, as well as remaining highly resistive to intervention. (Greater elaboration of this will be found in the section on Stage 1: Trust versus Mistrust versus Naïveté). The infant will take in facial expressions, tone of voice and even body movements—to be mimicked later on. At a different level, he will elaborate on the organizational structures and hierarchies in place, continuously modifying them. From a small, hundred-cell psychic raspberry, the images of "self" and "the world" and "the other" become multicluster raspberries all attached to one another, increasingly refined and defined and include up to one thousand representations—some larger and more dominant than others. Yet the others remain in the unconscious until they are "squeezed out" by further development or become residual feelings with no memory attached.

A significant dilemma occurs in that the infant will vacillate between fantasy (Klein's phantasy) and reality in these early months. When hungry, he can fantasize being fed. If hungry and he cries and no one comes, he can fantasize the destruction of the ungiving breast or mother. The range of fantasies is infinite and the infant has no way to discern reality from fantasy. Thus the dialectic between Klein and Bowlby (see pages forty and following) represents a lack of compromise on this issue so that contemporary science may soon document the validity of both propositions.

Our analysis of the mind at this point may carry us up through the first three or four months following birth. The mind continues differentiating, organizing and reorganizing, creating new hierarchies and—at times—creating temporary connections to allow more permanent ones to develop. It is here that the interface between intrapsychic life and external reality can be understood via the Psychosocial Theory of Erik Erikson.

CHAPTER 3

Erik Erikson and
Psychosocial Theory

Erikson's greatest innovations and contributions to psycho-analytic theory include three distinct elements: focusing on the interaction of the human psyche with the world, rather than internal processes alone; postulating eight stages of development, in contrast to Freud's five; and identifying the bimodal conflicts inherent to each stage of development.

The first, and perhaps most critical, point of Erikson's contribution lies in the fact that he understood and promulgated a theory that asserts that the individual stands inseparable from the society in which he is raised—hence, the designation Psychosocial Theory. Clinical evidence abounds to demonstrate how inseparable man is from the human society in which he grows, i.e., the multiple cases where a human being grew up in nonhuman society. In the 1970's came the case of Ramachandra. First reported in 1973, in the Uttar Pradesh region of India, living an amphibian lifestyle in the Kuano River, he was captured by scientists in 1979. He only partly adapted to a conventional life-style, continuing to prefer raw food, walking with an awkward gait, and spending most of his time alone in nearby rivers and streams.

In 1984, a seven-year-old girl was found by an Italian missionary in Sierra Leone. She apparently had grown up with chimps. "Baby" (her name) was unable to stand upright, crawled instead of walking, and ate directly from a bowl without using her hands. She made the chattering noises of apes or monkeys.

Her arms and hands were reported to be well developed, but not her leg muscles—as would be expected had she transported herself by swinging in trees instead of walking. She resisted attempts to civilize her, spending much of her time in an activity that is very unusual for feral children—crying. In the 1990's, Ivan Mishukov was found near Moscow. Reconstructing his history suggested he had been raised by dogs for two years and had risen to being "alpha male" of the pack. As late as 2007, Lyokha Kaluga had been living with a pack of wolves, had typical wolf like behavior and reactions. He was unable to speak any human language. Taken to a Moscow hospital, he received medical treatment, a shower, a nail trim and several meals before escaping from the building. He is believed to still be living in the wild. Also in 2007—in the United States—came the case of a child deprived of human contact for the first seven years of her life. Danielle Crockett demonstrates the results of such deprivation. Current efforts focus on acclimating her to human conditioning, including learning English and effective communication.

These instances (and hundreds of others) document the integrated psyche/society unity constituting the mind of man. Theory therefore needs to address the interaction of the individual with society if it means to delineate the causes of human thoughts, feelings and behavior.

From the perspective of theory, emphasizing the interaction of the individual with society does not detract from classic intrapsychic perspectives, such as phantasies, attachment, and oedipal conflicts, but rather extends and expands them—embedding them in a deeper more intricate analysis of the human mind.

Erikson's second great contribution, i.e., postulating eight stages of development in contrast to Freud's five, completely alters psychoanalytic thinking; yet it fits more with research findings—both psychological and sociological—than does classical psychoanalytic theory, i.e., the notion that development comes to a halt after pubescence. This emphasis on life span development opens psychoanalytic thinking to embrace a fuller range of human experience while not denigrating more traditional psychoanalytic thinking.

Finally, in proposing the unique bipolar conflicts marking each stage of development, Erikson directed the attention of psychoanalysis to the continuum of resolutions available at each stage—extending psychoanalytic thinking immeasurably. By promulgating the premise that a person must hold each specific life-stage challenge simultaneously in tension with one another—not rejecting one pole or the other—in order to achieve optimum mental health, Erikson moved psychoanalytic thinking from conceptualizing in a dichotomous mode (black-white thinking) to thinking along a continuum. He perceived that only when both extremes in a life-stage challenge are understood and accepted as both required and useful, can the optimal virtue for that stage surface. Thus, "trust" and "mistrust" must both be understood and accepted, in order for realistic "hope" to emerge as a viable solution at the first stage. Similarly, "integrity" and "despair" must both be understood and embraced, in order for actionable "wisdom" to emerge as a viable solution at the last stage.

Such a counterintuitive proposition indicates that Erikson himself laid the groundwork for considering a third outcome at each stage of development, said outcome representing the compromise and blend of the two extreme positions. For example, Basic Trust represents a compromise between Naiveté (blindly believing in and trusting others) and Mistrust (skeptical that anyone can be relied on). The expression of the trait at any point in time will depend on the "penetration of the trait" and particular situational circumstances in which the person finds himself. Erikson linked the ability to understand polar opposites at each stage to achieving the "virtue" potentially emanating from each stage. Thus, as an individual understands and embraces both "trust" and "mistrust," he will attain "hope" to emerge as a viable solution at the first stage.

For Erikson a cornerstone of life span development involves recapitulating earlier stages of development at each more advanced stage, i.e., every conflict associated with each stage of development reoccurs—and must be re-resolved at a higher level in later stages of development.

Between birth and one-year-old, the infant can develop Basic Trust in whatever representations (phantasies) he continually creates as the world imposes on him and he responds. As different phantasy images are created and stored, those that represent consistent experiences will be assigned to a cluster sharing some common elements—as defined by the infant. Thus, this goes beyond the "good-breast" versus "bad breast" mode. The infant can create five or eight phantasies that will remain quasi-independent of each other until he can synthesize those using higher level cortical elements.

Once the infant has attained a basic sense of Trust or Mistrust or has become Overly Trusting, he will face the issue of Trust at later stages. Typically between birth and one year of age, the focus of Trust is in the immediate care givers. When the infant becomes a Toddler, his sense of Basic Trust expands to include less familiar people. The noted rapprochement that occurs when the Toddler wanders away to be out of sight from his mother, but 'checks in' regularly to determine that she has not left, reflecting the balance of early Autonomy that the Toddler seeks and a Basic Trust in mother remaining and in the world being a friendly place—all of which adds to the internal representations (phantasies) that he has.

Between one and three years of age, that sense of Trust will extend to persons less directly involved in daily care (e.g., babysitters). Starting between ages three and four, the child must trust day care providers and school personnel. Preschool experiences and time away from primary caregivers for days or even a week at a time can occur—if the child has Basic Trust. During the latency phase (Industry versus Inferiority) the child develops trust in coaches, camp counselors and parents of friends. In late adolescence having Basic Trust (in self, as well as others) comes into play as the individual leaves for college or the Armed Forces or just to live on his own. In order for the young adult to become intimate, he must first have Basic Trust.

The ever expanding sense of Trust not only involves more people, but trusting at a deeper level. Developing trust will be resolved again and again through adolescence and lead to the Trusting that is involved in achieving Intimacy with another in a loving relationship—always with the potential that profound Mistrust can result from trauma. Between ages three and six, the child is faced with the task of further expanding Trust to include both a larger world (day care, preschool, etc,) and people who start off being absolute strangers. Between ages six and ten school personnel and team coaches and camp staff are added. For many individuals, attending high school represents a larger and more threatening audience. Going away to college entails moving to a different geographic location and a much larger universe to Trust—and creates a crisis of Identity for many. Each Eriksonian conflict (e.g., Autonomy, Initiative, and Industry) can be subjected to a similar analysis, i.e., the need for continuously integrating the conflict and resolving it at ever higher levels.

Neo-Eriksonian Theory

The redefinition of the challenges at each Eriksonian stage of development is provided below.

The Eight Ages of Man Expanded

Stage 1: Trust versus Mistrust versus Naïveté

Stage 2: Autonomy versus Self-Doubt versus Willfulness

Stage 3: Initiative versus Guilt versus Intrusiveness

Stage 4: Industry versus Inferiority versus Compulsivity

Stage 5: Identity versus Role Diffusion versus Foreclosure

Stage 6: Intimacy versus Isolation versus Superficiality

Stage 7: Generativity versus Stagnation versus Regression

Stage 8: Ego Integrity versus Despair versus Ego Dissolution

Each stage can be encapsulated by a succinct statement that represents a distilled meaning to the primitive brain.

Primary-Conscious Mode	Unconscious Mode
Stage 1 I am what I am given	I am what I accept/take
Stage 2 I am what I will	I have power
Stage 3 I am what I imagine I can be	I have unlimited potential
Stage 4 I am what I produce and learn	I invest energy
Stage 5 I am more than the sum of parts	I am who I am
Stage 6 I am myself shared with another	I continue to develop
Stage 7 I am what I contribute to the world	I open up to the world
Stage 8 I have peace	I am complete

This model implies continual differentiation of the human personality, paralleling embryological-fetal development and neurological-brain development. The end result produces the incredible diversity of human beings and the infinite variety of behaviors manifest to all every day. More importantly, such a model represents a first effort at a "unified theory of mind" that will account for that diversity.

CHAPTER 4

Stage 1: Trust versus
Mistrust versus Naïveté

Erikson postulates that during the first stage in human beings' psychosocial-emotional development the infant develops either a Basic Trust in the world (typically or especially the mother-provider) or—at the opposite extreme—learns to Mistrust. The infant will resolve this conflict more on the side of Basic Trust if he has his basic needs met when they arise or reasonably soon thereafter, leading to the infant mind creating a representation (phantasy) that the world is a trustworthy place peopled with need-meeting persons. Mistrust will result when—for whatever reason—the infant does not experience his basic needs (being fed, being held, being changed) being met. Naïveté occurs when an infant is over attended to with every whimper and every whim responded to immediately.

At this point in development, the individual can best be conceived as operating with all three brains contributing to behavior and feelings with the reptilian brain (black-white thinking, raw emotion) dominating functioning and having the most significant effect on the phantasies manufactured by the infant. As time goes on, the mammalian brain and later the neocortex will assume ever increasing control and direction of behavior, thoughts and feelings.

But Trust is a function of the cortex (or hominid brain); and, therefore, the infant will only develop Trust if the neocortex receives positive signals from the reptilian brain that survival is assured and his needs will be met, as well as from the mammalian brain that the developing representations are consistent.

Both the cortex and mammalian brain will store (in their respective memories) the combine of phantasies, memories and feelings so as to strengthen the representations that lead to the child having continual Trust.

This first year of life parallels Freud's Oral stage. During this period the mouth region provides great sensual satisfaction and a means of exploring and learning about the world to include developing Trust. Freud views the first six months as the time when the individual develops incorporativeness, i.e., seeking union with the world—which can define Bonding and Attachment. The second six months will reflect more aggressiveness (e.g., biting the breast) and exploratory behavior (i.e., putting everything in its mouth as though to test out whether the object will bring satisfaction, which will further refine the psychic representations, i.e., the infant proving to himself that biting will not lead to rejection or annihilation.)

Studying orality itself provides a focus for many hypotheses. An infant being breast-fed will likely develop a different inner representation than one being bottle-fed, but oversimplifying this process of bonding will not serve good psychoanalytic understanding. An infant being lovingly bottle-fed may develop more Trust than one being breast fed by a resentful or depressed mother since there will be greater conflict among the sensations the latter infant experiences leading to creating more diverse and confusing/conflicting memories and fantasies.

Physiologically whatever tendency the neocortex may have to develop Trust can be disrupted when the reptilian brain detects a similarity between a current representation being created and a prior situation (real or phantasied) that engendered Mistrust. If the similarity is strong enough the Unconscious will transcend time and return to the original representation and re-experience the original feelings. When an infant cries or expresses rage for no apparent reason, it suggests that he/she is living the representation, not the immediate situation. Any event, sound, color, touch, or smell can set off the representation.

Other psychoanalysts approached the issue of Trust from slightly different perspectives. John Bowlby, a British physician and psychoanalyst, working with different cultural and experiential groups produced his early work on the significance of the early years of development. By the late 1950s Bowlby had accumulated a body of observational and theoretical work to indicate the fundamental importance for human development of attachment from birth. He took the theory further when he proposed that attachment difficulties would be transmitted from one generation to the next and stood among the first to propose that lack of attachment produced maladapted and delinquent children. His Attachment and Loss trilogy set a foundation for understanding that the first two years of life provide the psychological base for developing Trust or developing Mistrust leading to severe depression or antisocial personality disorder. Bowlby's insistence that "maternal deprivation" significantly impacted the child's psychological development and future interpersonal relationships parallels Erikson's conception of Trust.

Bowlby proposed that the infant's real relationship with his mother (not phantasies) determined his intrapsychic life. He also attempted to differentiate between the effects of privation (no primary attachment figure) and deprivation (loss of the primary attachment figure)—a distinction that caused problems for other analysts. Critics maintained that he did not allow for the loss of a primary attachment figure and other forms of deprivation and under stimulation that may affect children in institutions or in impoverished environments.

Mary Ainsworth, a student of Bowlby's, elaborated on his ideas and proposed that several attachment styles existed (secure, anxious-ambivalent-insecure, and anxious-avoidant-insecure). A securely attached child will explore freely while the mother is present, will engage with strangers, will be visibly upset when the mother departs, and happy to see the mother return. Typically the child will not engage with a stranger if mother is not in the room. Therefore, secure attachment can be seen as the most adaptive attachment style with anxious-ambivalent and anxious-avoidant reflecting insecurity (and Mistrust). According to some psychological researchers, a child becomes securely attached when the mother is available and able to meet the needs of the child in a responsive and appropriate manner.

A fourth category (disorganized-disoriented) was added by Ainsworth's colleague Mary Main, and Ainsworth accepted the validity of this modification. Main describes this attachment thus: ". . . the child may cry during separation but avoid the mother when she returns or may approach the mother, then freeze or fall to the floor. Some show stereotyped behavior, rocking to and fro or repeatedly hitting themselves." Main and Hesse found that most of the mothers of these children had suffered major losses or other trauma shortly before or after the birth of the infant and had reacted by becoming severely depressed. In fact, fifty-six percent of mothers who had lost a parent by death before they completed high school subsequently had children with disorganized attachments.

Research about children establishes the immediate impacts of a lack of bonding or attachment (and attending implied Lack of Trust). Clinical case studies done well—one-at-a-time with individual patients—add to our understanding of the longer term, even lifetime, effects of the infant failing to establish a sense of Basic Trust. Historical research with adults (with all the difficulties involved) contributes a higher degree of insight. In a 1960 study of death row inmates (unpublished), authors Lewis and Pincus, seeking to ascertain how death row inmates differed from other prisoners, found no significant differences along more than fifty psychological and sociological dimensions. However, where they could find records, sixty-four percent of the cases of these sociopaths (an implied diagnosis) indicated a prolonged separation from the mother during the first year of life.

Another study—of men who had murdered more than one person—reported an informal observation that more than fifty percent of the murderers had a tattoo saying Mom or Mother while only twenty-two percent of other inmates had a similar tattoo. Psychoanalytic interpretation of such data implies the wish to retain a connection with the mother in a manner such that the individual could never again be separated from her.

Such research studies give credence to the significance of the first year of life and having the infant develop Trust—based on having a real figure to whom he can attach.—The findings allow us to infer general patterns, recognizing that individual differences exist that produce deviations from the general principle.

To develop Trust requires a basically reliable environment. A child will develop negative or faulty representations of the world and others, as well as of himself, leading to Mistrust if he does not have the experience of basic reliability. However, the opposite end of the spectrum also needs to be considered. What happens when the infant is not allowed to experience any frustration or delay? Is attended to every minute? Feelings of omnipotence develop; feelings of entitlement; and, by extrapolation, a sense of complete trust not only in the world, but in the inner sense of being able to handle any situation even if by magical thinking.

When children are exposed to a fundamentally healthy environment and their needs are met in some consistent fashion, they possess sufficient flexibility to develop with minor insecurities or frustrations. Lacking the opportunity to experience frustration or insecurity will lead to a different strand of character malformation, i.e., Naïveté.

At present psychological research has not focused on this particular issue. However, sociological observations and data come together to provide a global conception of issues that result from Naïveté. Studies conducted regarding population influx into Las Vegas indicate that four thousand people a month were moving into Las Vegas, but two thousand people a month were moving out—the majority of whom were the elderly who had retired there for the sunshine and ended up losing their life savings because they had accepted the hospitality of the casinos and trusted that such generous people would not harm them—Naïveté.

Analyzing the phenomenon of women who enter into and remain in abusive relationships suggests that they are Naïve, i.e., that they remain blind to warning signs and actual abuse, believing (naïvely) that the offender will change. The entire phenomenon of what is labeled codependency has at its base naïveté—too much trusting with no basis for trusting. Another example is the Naïveté that allows a parent to deny that that a child or spouse is using drugs or engaging in other illicit behavior.

Developing Basic Trust—neither Mistrust nor Naïveté—at this very early stage lays the foundation for trusting others at ever higher levels. As importantly—or even more importantly—developing trust in the world constitutes a prerequisite for an individual's learning to trust himself.

CHAPTER 5

Stage 2: Autonomy versus
Self-Doubt versus Willfulness

It starts when he first turns over. All who have witnessed it know the look that comes over a baby's face—a look of glee and power.

Thus begins the development of Autonomy. From that simple start, the baby will turn over again and again and again— each time creating in his brain the representations of the motor movements and the inner feeling of power. Turning over rapidly progresses to pushing himself up and from that to edging along the floor, then standing up (changing his world perception and self-perception immeasurably). Not unusually, by the end of the first year a child has taken steps and experienced the ability to propel himself without relying on someone else. With each step, his self-representation (phantasy) expands exponentially and with it the feeling of power and independence.

Between the end of the first year and the beginning of the third year of life—which Freudian theory labels the Anal stage—Erikson identifies a broader issue, the emergence of autonomy. The infant becomes a Toddler. He has started down the path towards independence. With his new motor and mental abilities, the child can walk, climb, open and close, drop, push and pull, hold and let go. He will learn to say "no"; decide he does not want to eat certain foods; and, at times, even resist getting dressed.

The Toddler will resolve the conflict relating to this stage of development–working towards autonomy—to the extent that he is allowed to fully experience his power and abilities (safely).

To the extent that he hears many unnecessary no's, is punished for exploring or seeking to explore or restrained (in a playpen, for example), he will develop self-doubt and deep feelings of shame. Finally, at the other extreme, a child will become willful when he faces no limitations or is not allowed to experience natural consequences for his behavior or if parenting figures surrender to his tantrums. Erikson, himself—again suggesting that each stage has three options for resolving the particular development conflict associated with that age—states: "It might be well to note, in addition, that too much autonomy can be as harmful as too little. I have in mind a patient of seven who had a heart condition. He had learned very quickly how terrified his parents were of any signs in him of cardiac difficulty. With the psychological acuity given to children, he soon ruled the household. The family could not go shopping, or for a drive, or on a holiday if he did not approve. On those rare occasions when the parents had had enough and defied him, he would get angry and his purple hue and gagging would frighten them into submissions."

Actually, this boy was frightened of this power (as all children would be) and was really eager to give it up. When the parents and the boy came to realize this, and to recognize that a little shame and doubt were a healthy counterpoise to an inflated sense of autonomy (willfulness), the three of them could once again assume their normal roles

At this point in development, the individual can still be conceived as operating with all three brains contributing to behavior and feelings though in a different proportion. The mammalian brain with its specialized cells assigned to file new experiences and an ever-increasing capacity for not only having the memories but for having the conscious awareness of feelings (and fantasies) associated with those memories assumes more power in directing the infant, diminishing the impact of the reptilian brain somewhat. The flashes of primal terrors or rages will be evidenced in tantrum behavior; however it gets expressed (head banging, striking other children, deliberate noncontrol of bowels, etc.). It

35

is this transfer that allows feelings such as attachment—desire for greater closeness with mother (or parenting figure)—to override other rage-based or self-seeking impulses, thus having the Toddler negotiate within himself regarding his behavior.

This physical evolution impacts the psychoemotional and psychosocial changes. Before the age of one, the majority of infant's representations and fantasies centered on and around others, his self-representations reflecting a reality of his limitations, i.e., "I am what I am given." Starting with the act of turning over and proceeding with each new power acquired, his self-representation becomes, "I am what I can do." In addition, with each new breakthrough, the Toddler expands his self-representation while his primal unconscious fantasies become richer, i.e., he imagines more of what he can do. The child takes pride in all new accomplishments and will want to do everything himself, whether it be pulling the wrapper off a piece of candy, selecting the vitamin out of the bottle or flushing the toilet.

This ability to imagine doing something oneself creates potential for conflicts. In Judith Rossner's novel *August,* the heroine, Dawn, reports to her analyst that when she was younger she tried to murder her sister (and hence felt inordinate lifelong guilt). The analytic probing that followed demonstrated effectively that Dawn's recall was, to say the least, flawed and that she had only imagined or wished she could murder her sister.

Two major issues of this age—toilet training and eating—fit naturally into the key development issue of autonomy. Achieving control over bodily functions (and obtaining secondary reinforcement from adults) will readily become an issue of pride for the child—or, conversely, a battleground where he can assert his will. Likewise with food and eating. These years are also the years that a child learns to feed himself, as well as to assert what foods he likes or does not like. The number of parents who have had carrots, spinach, milk or tomatoes (and every other food imaginable) spit at them by an 18-month-old may well be incalculable.

This stage represents a significant shift for caretakers—balancing the need to encourage the child's independence and self-confidence and his need to explore with insuring that he is safe, having him accept limitations on his exploring and his willfulness and recognizing the realities of convenience (I once had a patient who allowed her two-and-a-half-year old up to thirty minutes to dress herself).

What happens in this stage is that the caretakers' Unconscious primal issues will dictate how they address the Toddler's need for independence. If they (the caretakers) faced severe restriction and never consciously acknowledged that they were or felt restricted, they will unconsciously restrict their child. If, on the other hand, they themselves were not restricted—or, if restricted, came to recognize, through education or therapy, the negative impact of that restricting—they will achieve the balance of caretaking that will contribute to the child's healthy resolution of the conflict at this stage. When caretaking is consistently overprotective and criticism of "accidents" (whether these be wetting, soiling, spilling or breaking things) is harsh and unthinking, the child develops an excessive sense of shame with respect to other people and an excessive sense of doubt about his own abilities to control his world and himself. When caretakers ignore a child or do not establish clear limitations and expectations, the child will become willful. When caretakers are impatient and do for the child what he is capable of doing himself, they reinforce a sense of shame and doubt.

The healthy self-representations that a child should have as a result of experiences at this stage are, "I am what I will" and "I have power." If the child leaves this stage with less autonomy than shame or doubt, he will be handicapped in all future attempts to achieve autonomy in adolescence and adulthood. Contrariwise, the child who moves through this stage with his sense of autonomy buoyantly outbalancing his feelings of shame and doubt is well prepared to be autonomous at later phases in the life cycle. Again, however, the balance of autonomy to shame and doubt set up during this period can be changed in either positive or negative directions by later events.

If the child emerges from this stage with a sense of willfulness, he will be dominated at the core level (in the reptilian brain with its black-white thinking) by an internal message—"I am because I oppose," implying to himself "Therefore, if I do not oppose, I will cease to exist." Hence is created the creature we know as the Oppositional-Defiant Disorder, which is experienced as chronic Conduct Disorders in Adolescence. As adults, these individuals disregard or flaunt the law, rules and conventions and often routinely engage in criminal behavior—despite verbalizing a desire to not do so.

CHAPTER 6

Stage 3: Initiative versus Guilt versus Passivity

Freud designated the years between three and six as the Phallic Stage of development. During this time, the child seeks out the parent of the opposite sex as a provider of not just comfort, but sensual satisfaction and comes to regard the same sexed parent as a rival. Behavioral traits of seductiveness (charm) and competitiveness surge to the forefront. As the child discovers his genitalia and the pleasure that he can experience all on his own, he will alter his self-representation while developing fantasies centered around the opposite sex parent, often accompanied by fantasies of eliminating the rival for that parent's affection directly or indirectly.

Guilt associated with these fantasies will ensue.

Erikson extended the breadth and depth of the child's conflicts to include all activities the child pursued and the development of imagination. As the child attains mastery of his body, his mental development allows him to refine his perceptions and imagine even what he has not been exposed to. This will lead him to seek to pursue activities without being encouraged—or given permission—by the adults in his life.

During these years the child experiences spectacular expansions of his motor abilities, cognition, language, imagination and social life. His curiosity and drive leads him to demand to know and have his questions answered. This is the age of the famous endless question, "Why?" And his imagination expands even more rapidly. Everything becomes magical. The child will—if allowed to—extend far beyond the immediate sensory experience in front of him. For example, when my oldest grandson (Brendan) was just four, my daughter asked me why he took so long to brush his teeth. We literally watched him through the door, which we had left cracked open. Even before he put the toothpaste on the toothbrush, Brendan had turned the toothbrush into an airplane that in his hand zoomed up and down and around the bathroom with absolutely no concern for clean teeth.

The awareness of body pleasure (triggering unconscious fantasies), combined with increased imagination and self-directed activity, creates what Erikson sees as the key conflict for this age—initiative at one of its poles and guilt at the other. Children allowed to "waste time" brushing their teeth or pestering parents with the question "why", will feel—to use an adult-based word—validated, i.e., not only are they told it is okay to spend hours playing and to fall down and hurt their knees, they are encouraged to. When adults disparage activity or fantasy, the child extends that disparagement to all his activities and will develop a sense of guilt over even wanting to engage in activity.

In the second stage of development the child engaged in parallel play. In Stage 3 he will take the initiative to play on his own, interact with both peers and adults and even tell "tall tales" resulting from his primary process and imagination. All these behaviors reflect initiative.

At the opposite end of the spectrum is the possibility that a child will develop feelings of guilt. Feelings of guilt develop because a child recognizes that he is not perfect enough, i.e., he does not adhere to Societal/Parental rules and expectations and has fantasies that represent totally unacceptable impulses. Thus his guilt is grounded in multiple motivations. Evidence of feelings of guilt can be found in the child's fear of the dark and expressing fear that parents may die, continuing to depend unduly on adults and negative self-statements.

The third alternative resolution that can occur during this stage is that a child will learn to be passive. He will not initiate activity, nor will he feel guilt. Passivity combined with a lack of guilt can lead to depending on charm (seductiveness) to be accepted and rejecting guilt (or the healthy aspect of regret better referred to as remorse). If he is cute enough, fun enough or smart enough, he derives a sense that he does not have to live by the rules of society—a starting block for developing sociopathic tendencies. Observing children in kindergarten or other social settings can provide an awareness of this development of charm and seductiveness.

During this time a dramatic shift occurs in the intrapsychic representations of the child. Sexual feelings and desires are driven underground (into the Unconscious) taking with them the fantasies of eliminating the competition (dad or brothers, mom or sisters). In many normal circumstances for boys, the Unconscious decision is to identify with the father; and the child may begin walking in an exaggerated way, seeking to eat food off father's plate or hold a cigarette in his hand—all reflecting this drive to imitate. In December 2009, a five-year-old boy was found wandering the streets of Atlanta holding an open can of beer in his hand (having already consumed half of it). When asked about his behavior, the boy replied that he thought if he did this he could go to jail to be with his daddy. For girls, becoming more attuned with how mother comports herself, helping with kitchen work or housekeeping chores or just wanting time with mother is common. In encountering more people, the child will develop representations of them while modifying existing representations he or she has.

The greatest expansion, however, is of the self-representation. Having an imaginary playmate symbolizes a child's manufacturing from Unconscious material "the perfect companion," who often possesses qualities that the child himself does not have. When allowed, the child will allow himself to diversify, i.e., behave in ways that are seemingly inconsistent. (This is also a result of the continued impact of the mammalian and reptilian brain on behavior and feelings.) At times he will be able to share or take turns and at other times he will refuse to do so—violently. He may come up to give mother/caregiver a hug and five minutes later scream, "I hate you" to her. Seeking frequent

41

adult approval is counterbalanced by an "I don't care attitude." Observing the role-playing and imaginative games of children this age provides the clues to much of what is going on.

All three brains continue contributing to behavior and feelings though the influence of the reptilian brain decreases dramatically and the mammalian brain and cortex assume primacy of operation—unless special circumstances prevail. Unconscious material will still break through with regularity. However, the tantrum behavior and physical aggression of the Toddler (reptilian dominance) surrenders to the verbal aggression (mammalian brain consciousness of and control of feelings) by the preschooler. Name-calling and taunting become tools by which to establish superiority and exclude others.

It is impossible to leave discussion of this stage of development without commenting on the subject of Transitional love objects (pacifiers, blankets, teddy bears, etc.) These objects hold deep emotional meaning for the child—they represent an unconscious awareness of the love that the child felt he had then lost—or never had at all but wished he had had from mother. Such interpretation deepens our understanding of why children can react so strongly to the "loss" of a seemingly trivial object.

CHAPTER 7

Stage 4: Industry versus Inferiority versus Compulsivity

Most American and Western European children enter school at age six where, for the ensuing five years, they compete with dozens of other children for attention—a far cry from the individual attention they may have had at home—and face the demands to learn and to perform. These five years require that the child transform his initiative, which focused on play and imagination and social skills, into a sense of industry at one end of the continuum or, at the other end, a sense of inferiority. Added to Erikson's conception—again implied by his later writing—is a third branch of this conflict representing the child becoming compulsive, i.e., "I am what I produce." Industry will lead to a sense of competence; compulsivity leads more to a sense of mindless (and soulless) efforts to produce.

This is the age of Lemonade stands, selling Girl Scout cookies or candy for the Mission Trip or washing cars—all contribute to a sense of Industry. The activity of the prior stage has added to it an emphasis on the product of the activity. One child might select working for the Church or Boy Scouts as a means to express his industriousness. Team sports focus a child's industry with the product being "winning" and being the league champion, while along the way, the children establish a sense of superiority (or inferiority). With children at younger ages, coaches and leagues tend to operate with a policy of letting everyone have playing time. As children get older, however, the emphasis is on having the more skilled athletes playing most, if not all, of a game. Other competitive games (Chutes and Ladders, Scrabble, etc.) serve the same purpose.

At earlier ages—six to nine—children tend to see rules as rigid and unbreakable. Whether in sports or other endeavors, the famous phrase "It's not fair" becomes part of the repertoire of almost every child. Children know that even in school there are rules in school and can become very upset if the rules are not enforced consistently—leading to the infamous tattletale syndrome.

In the later phases of this stage—ages nine to twelve—children work to modify the rules or devise their own rules.

In most United States homes, industry implies a stress on academic achievement and performance. Industry, however, transcends academics and sports and lemonade stands. On the personal level, children strive to learn "how things work," including toys, machines, their own bodies, etc. They will take things apart (and not always put them back together). The emphasis is on the working behind the product or activity. In many homes the emphasis becomes "how this family works," meaning the inner workings of obedience and rewards and personal relationships. This age represents an excellent time to assign chores to children—if for no other reason except for the child to learn responsibility and contributing to the family.

Freud labeled this era the latency era based on the notion that during this time the child's attachment to the parent of the opposite sex and rivalry with the same sexed parent (elements in the so-called family romance) become suppressed, and then repressed, allowing the child to turn his attention to sports and academics and games.

When children are encouraged in their efforts to make, do or build practical things (whether it be to construct creepy crawlers, tree houses or airplane models—or to cook, bake or sew), are allowed to finish their products and are praised and regarded for the results, then the sense of industry is enhanced. But parents who see their children's efforts at making and doing as "mischief" and as simply "making a mess" help to encourage in children a sense of inferiority.

Whether the child develops a sense of industry or inferiority, however, no longer depends solely on the caretaking efforts of the parents but on the actions and offices of other adults as well. With the expansion of his world, the child interacts with teachers and coaches and youth leaders—any one of whom can play a central role in helping the child resolve this psychosocial conflict in favor of industry.

What the child experiences in school will impact his sense of inferiority. If he does not do well in school, he will most probably develop a sense of inferiority. Some academically challenged children emphasize their athletic prowess as a means of compensating for their lack of abilities. Others resort to being charming or funny or troublemakers.

The third resolution possible at this stage can be labeled compulsivity. Compulsivity occurs when the child begins to define himself (and elaborates on this during later stages of development) exclusively by what he produces. Often those who choose this path are identified as overachievers. Compulsivity will often be encouraged by adults and society. Gymnastics provides one great example. The success of the Romanian and Russian Gymnastics programs in producing Olympic champions led others to follow suit and have young children spend tireless hours striving to achieve perfection. Mark Spitz spent eight hours a day swimming. Figure skaters often do the same. Tiger Woods's father had him practice how many shots every day?

There is no question that compulsivity can readily lead to Identity Foreclosure (See the following stage). During this stage, the neocortex (hominid brain) establishes dominant control over thinking, behavior and feelings. The mammalian brain's contribution continues to focus on building memories of "what works" and increasing conscious recognition of feelings. Major behavior traits developed during this period include

Lawrence Dugan, Ph.D.

conscience (or the internalization of parental and societal moral and ethical demands) and compulsivity, setting the stage for Adolescence and the stage that Erikson recognized as pivotal in an individual's establishing a lifelong Identity.

CHAPTER 8

Stage 5: Identity versus Role Diffusion versus Pseudoidentity

(Ages thirteen–sixteen)

E rikson defined identity thus: "a subjective sense as well as an observable quality of personal sameness and continuity, paired with some belief in the sameness and continuity of some shared world image. As a quality of unselfconscious living, this can be gloriously obvious in a young person who has found himself as he has found his communality. In him we see emerge a unique unification of what is irreversibly given—that is, body type and temperament, giftedness and vulnerability, infantile models and acquired ideals—with the open choices provided in available roles, occupational possibilities, values offered, mentors met, friendships made, and first sexual encounters." (1970)

The physiological changes of pubescence precipitate dramatic changes in the child's psyche. The biological upheaval taking place on the inside manifests in the moods, words and actions on the outside. The sweet, considerate and obedient twelve-year-old becomes a devil possessed, inconsiderate, disobedient, and argumentative thirteen-year old, sometimes instantaneously and at other times gradually. Clinical researchers openly state that—by adult criteria—fifty percent of all adolescents would qualify as mentally disturbed—a reflection of the cognitive and emotional chaos that marks the early phase of this stage. This "breaking down" of the childhood personality signals that the flood of hormones has impacted the alignment of the three brains and that—however temporarily—the reptilian brain functions (black-white thinking, sexual drive, need to dominate) re-emerge as the force directing thoughts, feelings and behavior.

Freudian theory asserts that during these years the individual re-experiences an awakening of the family-romance problem of early childhood, which will lead the young person to start the search for a partner to explore his genital sexuality, with sexual release as a clear goal. Whereas in former years this held true more for boys, in recent years girls, too, have sought sexual exploration and release as part of their identity.

Erikson's definition delineates a number of core elements facing the young person striving to create an identity:

- Accepting one's physique and other attributes—building self-esteem
- Achieving healthy, more mature social relations with others
- Defining a masculine or feminine social role for themselves
- Achieving emotional independence from parents and other adults
- Preparing for their future personal life (marriage and family, for example)
- Preparing for an economic career
- Defining the values they will use as a guide to behavior, including desiring and achieving socially responsible behavior.

The process of forming an identity demands blending the experiences from each stage with the internal feelings and representations of those experiences into a unified, relatively coherent oneness. By the end of this stage, the individual believes in his/her capacity to sustain inner sameness and continuity of thinking that matches the perceptions of others, i.e., other people will communicate that they perceive a sameness and continuity in the person that then reassures the developing individual that there is indeed a core of self that others experience.

The now teenager has new tools to aid his task as he develops cognitively—including the ability to abstract; he works at creating his "sense of self" unfettered by, or even rejecting of, prior ideas he or his family may have promoted. He focuses on life issues important to him with a new capacity to look at and think about the world. He may reexamine his beliefs about his family. He may become preoccupied with what others—especially peers—think of him and can wonder about how they think. Finding a peer group with whom he can "be himself" becomes a priority. The young adolescent begins "playing with" the ideas of different careers for himself—at times changing his mind daily. Often—due to the sexual reawakening he experiences—the young adolescent searches for a special partner—physically desirable and adoring of them—to explore the boundaries of romance.

The label "role diffusion"—for Erikson—represents a crisis for a person and can lead to lacking an identity—a sense of not knowing what he is, where he belongs or to whom he belongs. This, in turn, can lead to the individual's being susceptible to other influences, such as joining a gang, forming a negative identity by engaging in delinquent behavior or opting out (becoming a pothead or an alcoholic). Without a core identity, a person will have an amoeba-like character—lacking structure and purpose, regardless of intelligence or cognitive sophistication. A classic sociological example is provided by the individual who is "good at everything" but never settles on one definitive path to express his or her talents and personality. A child of wealthy parents who has been allowed to step into a family business or other role without being party to that decision is one example. A young person who spends seven years at college and lacks a degree is another. (Research findings reveal that more than fifty percent of college students change majors at least five times and that the average college student requires five and a half years to complete a degree.)

Pseudoidentity formation refers to that distinct phenomenon whereby the individual takes a role assigned by others (or his fantasies about what others expect), i.e. the adolescent "caves in" to pressures leading him to follow a path that is not his and to which he will not commit with all his internal resources. Pseudoidentity involves the individual's belief that "others know better" or that "I can do this." Those who resolve the identity crisis by the path of Pseudoidentity present with characteristics that in adults would be identified as passive-dependent personality or masochistic personality traits.

Even in present times, many young women pursue marriage and being a mother rather than seeking to develop an identity—because that is what is encouraged by their family of origin. The individual who graduates from college and "takes over the family business" rather than pursuing his own career is another. One example can be found in the case of a man of Chinese descent who graduated with a degree in architecture and computer programming and who, for fifteen years after he graduated, operated the chain of five restaurants for his family because "that is what the oldest son does."

Researcher James Marcia (1966, 1976, 1980) has expanded on Erikson's theory, specifically identifying different identity statuses, among them Identity Foreclosure whereby a person makes a commitment without exploring options. Clinically, this phenomenon represents the emphasis of certain sectors of society as cited in the prior chapter with the example of young gymnasts, figure skaters, Mark Spitz, Tiger Woods and how many hundreds—if not thousands—of other athletes, beauty pageant contestants and young actors and actresses. Sociologically it represents situations where a young person willingly chooses (for healthy reasons) to enter the family business at the age of twelve or thirteen. Identity Foreclosure represents an option—not necessarily an unhealthy one—for an individual and family to consider.

For the most part, in the years between thirteen and sixteen, an individual will assemble dozens of pieces to create ego identity. When the child reaches adolescence having achieved a healthy balance of earlier stages (a vital sense of trust, autonomy, initiative and industry), he will have a much greater probability of putting together all he has felt about being a son, brother, friend, worker, teammate, boyfriend, student and worker and of seeing himself as unique, one of a kind—that is his identity.

These dimensions challenge the teenager to emerge from this period with a sense of Ego Identity. At the opposite end (negative) of Erikson's bipolar scheme is a sense of role-confusion. Individuals who do not fit into a certain social group (brainiacs, athletes, punkers, artists, etc.) can emerge as "loners." They place themselves in no social context. While there is a healthy balance between identifying with a group and maintaining one's individuality, loners are those who do not "fit in." On the positive side, they can end up being the eccentric genius; on the negative side, they can traverse an entirely different path. Throughout this stage of development, the individual continues to shape and reshape his or her sense of identity and autonomy—autonomy not just from thinking and being exactly as his family of origin was, but also from any undue groupthink, regardless of the group. Here the adolescent employs his newfound integrative abilities to bring together everything he has learned about himself as a son, student, athlete, friend and worker, and integrate these different components and images into a self-chosen unit. He establishes his sense of psychosocial identity with awareness of who he is, where he has been and where he is going. Healthy individuals make the connection between present behavior and future consequences and potentials.

CHAPTER 9

Stage 6: Intimacy versus Isolation versus Superficiality

(Ages seventeen–thirty-five)

Arguably Erikson's most significant contribution to understanding human development lies in extending the concept of development and the developmental challenges beyond the age of puberty. In doing so, Erikson challenges the core of Freudian thinking and offers a mode of understanding the intricacies of man in modern society.

Stage Six in the Eriksonian life cycle is young adulthood—roughly the period from dating through courtship and early family life, which extends from late adolescence till early middle age. Erikson asserted that attaining a sense of personal identity and engaging in productive work during this time parallels a more significant development—the rise of a new interpersonal dimension of intimacy at the one extreme and isolation at the other.

When Erikson speaks of intimacy, he intends a great deal more than love-making alone; he includes the ability to share with and care about another person without fear of losing oneself in the process. Intimacy involves deep friendships as well as romance. Soldiers who have served together under the most dangerous circumstances often develop a commitment to one another that exemplifies intimacy in its greatest sense. Many siblings—having comfortably established individual identities—develop intimate connections with one another. In Erikson's view, if intimacy is not established with friends or in a marriage, the individual will feel isolation—a sense of being alone with no one to share with or care for.

In basic Eriksonian thinking, at the polar opposite from Intimacy is Isolation. Isolation results from a variety of sources and manifests itself in many ways. When a person fears losing his identity in the act of becoming close to another, he will—albeit unconsciously—isolate himself. An individual stuck in an earlier stage of development (e.g., Industry) will lack the maturity to become intimate and thereby—by default—isolate himself from a genuine relationship. Other fears—including the fear of feeling anything—will drive many, especially men, into isolating and rationalizing the isolation (as described in *The Hazards of Being Male*).

The processes of isolation—often accompanied by higher level defenses—are varied. An individual will isolate himself by becoming a workaholic or following a career path limiting opportunities for closeness with others. Extreme competition serves to isolate a person by fostering attitudes of mistrust justified under the rubric of aggressiveness and "getting ahead." Seeking "someone perfect" allows the individual not only to isolate, but to complain about being isolated. The movie *Nine and a Half Weeks* creates a haunting picture of a man who lives in isolation—self sufficient to a ridiculous degree. The success of that movie reflects both its portrayal of current urban reality and the fact that it represents a fantasy to which many—both men and women—aspire.

Sociological research and clinical observations of young adults dictate identifying a third option at this stage of development, superficiality—or pseudointimacy. Scientific advances in preventing pregnancy (contraception) coupled with the reduced impact of religious and moral values on the lives of young people when accompanied by increased mobility and anonymity makes superficiality easy. Those seeking superficiality will often mask that drive by being pseudointimate, a process best represented by the prevalence of the sociological phenomenon known as "hooking up"—engaging in a physical relationship with no

other involvement between the two people. Lest anyone miscon-
strue the meaning of the term "physical," I offer the following
definition from novelist/satirist Tom Wolfe, "a spontaneous,
nonconversational, usually emotionless, apparently meaningless and definitely commitment free sexual encounter, typically
at a social gathering where alcohol or other intoxicants serve as
catalysts."

Wolfe, in his satirical anthology *Hooking Up*, compares
contemporary vocabulary to the now passé baseball analog in
which "first base" once designated an embrace or kiss, and a
"home run" meant having sexual intercourse: In the year 2000,
which we will designate as the era of hooking up, "first base"
meant deep kissing ("tonsil hockey"), groping and fondling;
"second base" meant oral sex; "third base" meant going all the
way; and "home plate" meant learning each other's names. The
contemporary emphasis on sexual freedom and sexual experi-
mentation reflected by "hooking up"—outside of moral consid-
erations—serves to prevent mentally healthy development, i.e.,
prevents people from learning to become intimate.

To presume that any young man or woman will choose to
have no or only one sexual partner between the ages of sixteen
and thirty can reflect naïveté (though, in actuality, many still
choose to do so). Nonetheless for a couple to engage in sexual
intimacy after being together for a year or more is—from a
psychological perspective—totally different from the psycho-
dynamics of "hooking up," where people engage in sexual activity in a manner that can best be considered whimsical.

This phenomenon of "hooking up" continues to grow despite
the fact that—according to considerable research—young women
have not surrendered the desire for a meaningful relationship. A
study by the Institute for American Values found that eighty-
three percent of undergraduate women report that "being married is a very important goal" for them. This statistical finding is
not a bias, based solely on the organization funding the research;
from the other side of the political fence, Nancy Pfotenhauer,
president of the Independent Women's Forum, was quoted in a

July 26, 2001, *Washington Post* article as saying: "Young women are trying more and more to act like men, but the problem is they don't react like men." She cites a study that found that a majority (sixty percent) of women report that "hooking up" makes them feel desirable—but also awkward, vulnerable, remorseful and hurt. (Psychoanalysis with those individuals would indubitably reveal multiple negative motivators dictating their decision.)

Clinical vignettes from psychoanalysis reveal how some people operate on a pseudointimate level—even to the point of marrying and having children—while never becoming truly intimate with anyone.

Prelude to Intimacy

Achieving intimacy represents such a quantum leap from earlier stages of psychoemotional development that it demands deeper understanding than earlier stages. Etching the representation of intimacy into the reptilian brain starts during fetal development and proceeds throughout the first year following birth. The process of mother-infant bonding creates the substrate on which both the cognitive image of intimacy and the emotional capacity for intimacy can grow. During these sixteen months (the final four months of pregnancy and the first twelve months of life) the infant blends thousands of experiences to construct representations (images) of "intimacy." These emotionally grounded images eventually commingle with the cognitive images the infant has created (images of "self" and "other") residing in both the reptilian and mammalian brains. If an individual does not have the opportunity to bond with a caregiver during that time, theory suggests he will fail to achieve true intimacy as an adult.

The ultimate inner representations of intimacy do not result solely from these primal images or emerge from purely ethereal fantasy. Beyond the first year of life, the person continues to experience and observe thousands of interactions that lead to his creating representations of intimacy (real or wished-for), which he then sets in the hominid-mammalian brain and strives to superimpose on his more primal representations in the reptilian brain. The individual, who, as a child, witnessed parents being respectful and kind to one another, touching and hugging and kissing often, constructs a model of intimacy that differs radically from that of the individual who, as a child, witnessed his father beating his mother as he tells her he loves her.

Whatever images the individual creates lie dormant in the later stages of the child's development. Then, during the biological development accompanying pubescence the images reemerge (at all three levels of the brain). The degree to which the individual has resolved Oedipal/Electra phantasies will determine how readily the individual transitions from this phase to the Intimacy stage of development and seeks an appropriate love object.

One final consideration regarding the components essential for an individual to achieve genuine intimacy lies in the development of the individual himself. Achieving intimacy demands healthy resolution of all earlier stages of development. Analyzing each earlier stage reveals the barriers it creates to a person becoming intimate. When an individual lacks Basic Trust, he will fail to achieve intimacy since—regardless of his conscious state of mind—his unconscious need for self-preservation will perceive danger in investing in another. A person who has not resolved developmental issues of Autonomy will—out of Shame and Self-Doubt—seek fulfillment in having another direct him and take responsibility for his actions. Guilt—grounded in the Oedipal/Electra complex, as well as in other early developmental issues—often drives the decision to find a partner and the choice of a partner. The dynamic of seeking a partner with superior attributes as a means of compensating for feelings of Inferiority has been documented hundreds of times in research and clinical experience. Finally, a person needs to possess a genuine identity in order to become intimate, secure in the knowledge that he and his partner can have different opinions and values, pursue separate interests (within limits) and express himself without fear.

Similar analyses can be applied to the opposite extremes along the spectrum of developmental issues. For example, persons whose resolution of Industry versus Inferiority settles at the Compulsive end of the spectrum will be so controlling that an intimate relationship lies beyond their grasp. Many analysts—David Elkind among them—argue that women seek intimacy first, then their own identity. Research provides a little support for that premise. However, from the perspective of developmental theory, the argument can be made that a woman's seeking intimacy first results directly from her not having had adequate emotional sustenance from her father and her need to resolve earlier issues—including residual components of the Electra complex. This is one form of Pseudoidentity formation that by all reports does not lead to creating an enduring intimate connection. On the other hand, women will often choose a potential partner who represents what is anathema to her parents—as a means of rebelling. This, too, constitutes pseudoidentity formation and, as such, will not lead to genuine lasting intimacy.

At this juncture in development the individual still experiences the vagaries of adolescent development regarding values, career choice and remaining independent while reconnecting to family. Whatever initial explorations of romance have occurred often becomes rejected as childish as the young person seeks genuine intimacy—without necessarily being able to define what intimacy means. There is a clash between late adolescent narcissism and idealism. His search for "the idealized other" who will reflect back his own self-love and glorification takes place in a context of not wanting to repeat whatever limitations the individual perceived in his family of origin.

Fueled by hormones, the biological imperatives drive the young person to seek physical intimacy. In healthy young people the sexual intimacy is accompanied by intellectual intimacy, i.e., the sharing of ideas and pursuit of knowledge, exploring philosophy, etc. that developed during adolescence. Joining these two to finalize the triumvirate of intimacy is emotional intimacy—two people as equals sharing feelings and doubts, plans, hopes and fears with another who is perceived as an equal (and loves the individual as much as the individual loves himself/herself). Such an intimacy requires both Trust and Autonomy trust in the other person's caring for us and independence in making the choice.

In addition, however, the notion of sacrifice, i.e., placing another's needs above one's own, stands at the core of intimacy. Erikson asserts that genuine intimacy can occur only when the ego has established mastery over the sexual drives of adolescence and achieved the ability to delay gratification. In addition, the person must confront the fear of "losing himself" in situations that may call for self-sacrifice or self-abandonment. For many young people in today's society—both men and women—the fear of feelings presents a block to genuine intimacy.

As mentioned above, the physiological upheaval associated with pubescence resets the balance of brain and reptilian brain functions (black-white thinking, sexual drive, need to dominate) re-emerge as the force directing thoughts, feelings and behavior. This, in turn, can lead to reawakening primal connections and ties of unresolved desires dating all the way back to infancy—including oedipal issues. Such an imbalance can lead a person (unconsciously) to seek out a love object for all the wrong reasons. Thus, for example, women who as girls who did not receive love from their fathers will unconsciously seek out a man who will not give them love. If they saw mother in an abusive relationship and unconsciously wished they could have stepped in to protect her, they will find and stay with an abusive male.

The skills that must emerge from this stage of development imply developing relationship skills and being open to sharing with others, healthy interactions with the opposite sex, and respect for self and others and self-discipline, unquestionably attributes that provide the foundation for a solid marriage—which, over time, demands ever-increasing intimacy.

CHAPTER 10

Stage 7: Generativity versus Self-Absorption versus Regression

(Ages thirty-five–sixty-five)

In 1900 the average life expectancy for a man was forty-seven years. Thus studying or theorizing about what we now term middle adulthood (ages forty—?) did not enter into academic consideration. As a scientific endeavor, life-span developmental psychology started evolving circa 1950—and, more or less, started with Erik Erikson. By that year, life expectancy had risen to 68.2. The term "middle-aged" became truly representative of an identifiable sociological phenomenon, including the recognition that those in this group represented a hitherto unstudied phenomenon. The Freudian notion—and Freud up through the 1960's and 1970's still held sway over significant numbers of social scientists—that development stopped after adolescence precluded psychologists and others from researching this group. As that sway dissipated and Eriksonian Theory attracted both academic and clinical attention, impetus to learn about this population sprang from the social sciences as well as marketing research.

This stage of development—from a true middle age towards old age—brings the person to what Erikson designates as either Generativity versus Self-absorption and Stagnation versus Regression.

Generativity in the Eriksonian scheme refers to that attitude whereby the individual extends his concerns beyond his immediate family to future generations and to the world that those generations will inhabit. Generativity reflects the mentally healthy individual who sees beyond himself and knows that he must contribute to making the world a better place and members ofhis family better citizens of the world. As such, it is not restricted to those who have children themselves.

Achieving a healthy resolution at this stage in life requires investing energy in others through multiple vehicles (Coaching young people, volunteering for social service, going on mission trips, being a Big Brother, etc.) Healthy resolution also will involve developing a broader sense of intimacy with one's partner, limiting interference in the lives of one's children, caring for aging parents to the point of role reversal, developing the nonwork aspects of oneself and a host of other specific tasks reflecting the expansion of one's world.

This arena of development in particular can be presaged by earlier experiences. Many teenagers start being assistants for the Little League Baseball Team or Peewee Football or Soccer Leagues, or referees or umpires where they learn that they take responsibility for those who are to follow them and they do so because they are asked by an adult who is himself or herself giving to that future generation.

For Erikson the opposite of Generativity, at the other end of the spectrum, is Self-absorption, people interested in and investing predominantly in their personal needs and comforts. Elkind uses as an example Scrooge in *A Christmas Carol*, who is so focused on his money that he disregards the needs of his sole employee and of charities in general. In Dickens' tale, Scrooge transformed from an embittered old man to a man invested in the future of someone else's progeny and actually developed a sense of intimacy very late in life. The contemporary movie *Scrooged* presents an excellent modern day version of this tale with the implied redemption.

Self-absorption is not always so readily overcome. In fact, it may be rare. Executives of firms who, like Bernie Madoff, bilked thousands of others to pad their own pockets—none of whom experienced the three ghosts of Christmas—could (literally, not just figuratively) have sailed off into the sunset unmindful of needs other than their own with no negative consequences. Aging rock stars and movie stars in recent headlines present two distinct pictures contrasting Generativity versus Stagnation —one set seeking continuous narcissistic feed and attention by engaging in excessive indulgence, the other demonstrating Generativity by finding some way to "make a difference", i.e., doing concerts to generate funds to preserve the Amazon, sponsoring foster homes for Save the Children, etc.

There also exists another process by which people choose stagnation as a solution to this stage. These individuals retreat every night to the world of television (or a personal hobby). In developmental terms, this reflects a high potential for an early descent into the Despair of Erikson's Eighth Stage.

A third option for individuals at this stage is Regression. Regression refers to the phenomenon whereby the individual retreats to an earlier stage of life, partially as a denial of the aging process and partially as a reflection of other unresolved issues. One notable example is Woody Allen, who in this phase decided to marry a fourteen-year-old girl—indubitably reflecting where his own psychoemotional development arrested. Other more plebian examples include men who divorce at this stage to marry women ten to fifteen years younger because they "finally found someone who 'listened' to them"—more a reflection of their own developmental failure to have chosen the correct healthy partner during the Intimacy phase than a flaw in the partner per se. (Recent statistics indicate that women, too, seek to end a marriage that is a marriage in name only based on a desire for true intimacy and a recognition that they chose the wrong partner.) Other individuals go back even further (e.g., to the Identity Formation stage) to "reinvent" themselves and find a new career, etc.

Understand that not all such endeavors must be considered unhealthy. If, for example, a man entered a career under family pressure or "only for the money," that career choice did not reflect his true identity. In such an instance, the regression, though perhaps uncomfortable for his immediate family, represents a mentally healthy search. I have had patients who stopped practicing law in order to become school teachers, social workers, etc. I have worked with an equal number of school teachers who left teaching to become attorneys—or musicians.

The rise in the divorce rate reflects how people may unconsciously select the wrong partner. Later in life the married person "falls in love" when he/she recognizes the error of choice and either feels a need to repeat the same mistake or gets good psychotherapy. Good psychotherapy does not cause divorce; it merely helps people realize that they made a mistake that is correctable—though at a cost.

This stage—more so than others—requires achieving balance in one's use of time and resources. There may be times when one spouse will object to how much the partner is extending for others, leaving insufficient time for the partnership or giving away too much money. This, too, represents the virtue of "caring" that Erikson sees as the natural result of successfully resolving issues at this stage.

CHAPTER 11

Stage 8: Ego Integrity versus Despair versus Escapism

The Eighth Stage in the Eriksonian Schema corresponds roughly to the period between the ages of 60 and 117 (the age of the oldest known individual in recent history). This era represents the age when an individual's major efforts and energies slow. As Rabbi Kushner states in his book *When Everything You Wanted Isn't Enough*, "It is a time to be with good friends to drink good wine." There is time for reflection—and for the enjoyment of family and friends. Literature and observations abound about the relationships that grandparents can have with their grandchildren. Recently I noted that many companies and organizations offer special travel packages for grandparents and grandchildren—reflecting their recognition of social reality. The psychosocial dimension that emerges into prominence now has—in Erikson's conceptualization—ego integrity on one hand and despair on the other.

Achieving Ego Integrity springs from the individual's ability to review his life with a sense of satisfaction that he used his talents, contributed to his family and society and—along the way—enjoyed any number of personal experiences (trips, golf, etc.) At the other extreme is the individual who looks back upon his life as a series of missed opportunities and missed directions. Facing the twilight years he begins to believe that it is too late for him. Such a person will manufacture a sense of despair at what might have been—what he did not do.

Examining what research there is and the tales of those who best reflect Ego Integrity leads to considering those whose most noted accomplishments occurred after age sixty, like Ray Kroc or Grandma Moses. The retired toll taker who designed the Tappan Zee Bridge. The ninety-three-year-old who finished third in a state wide skiing championship (open to all skiers over the age of sixty). The eighty-one-year old woman who earned her pilot's license. All these individuals represent examples of what is meant by ego integrity.

The television show *The Golden Girls* stands out as a breakthrough in that it portrayed women nearing sixty in new ways—addressing issues of the immanence of death, sex in senior citizens, careers and friendships and regrets. Two recent movies, *The Bucket List* and *Second Hand Lions* (A True Story), challenge simplistic notions regarding those over sixty years of age.

For this age, the alternative to Ego Integrity lies in the feeling of despair. In 1989 both *Time* and *Newsweek* published articles concerning the incidence of suicide among the elderly (300% greater than most other age groups—15.3 deaths/100,000 people). The statistic runs counter to our intuition. Such a statistic belies the image (as often portrayed on television) of the older couple hand-in-hand, walking together down a flower lined path. Other epidemiological research indicates that thirty percent or more of the elderly are on some form of antidepressant. Taken together, these numbers reflect the high degree of despair evident in those over sixty.

From a psychoanalytic perspective the emergence of feelings of despair at this juncture in life seems almost logical. An individual may have avoided unresolved developmental issues and conflicts throughout his life by focusing on his job, earning money, his family, raising children and getting them started in their own lives. At sixty, most of that is past. At sixty, that individual has no place to hide from whatever demons lie inside. In *Childhood and Society* Erikson states: "Every adult, whether he is a follower or a leader, a member of a mass or of an elite, was once a child. He was once small. A sense of smallness forms a substratum in his mind, ineradicably. His triumphs will be measured against this smallness, his defeats will substantiate it. The questions as to who is bigger and who can do or not do this or that, and to whom—these questions fill the adult's inner life far beyond the necessities and the desirability's which he understands and for which he plans." In the absence of "something to do," depression and despair take over.

Considering Ego Integrity the compromise position, with the extreme of despair at one end of the continuum, suggests that the other extreme can be labeled escapism. Escapism can assume many forms, both positive and negative, including developing chronic illnesses and interfering in the lives of children on the negative side. More positive resolutions include volunteerism, falling in love dedicating oneself even more to the next generation and becoming spiritually directed. The movie *Harold and Maude* illustrates one aspect of positive escapism. Maude, an eighty-year-old woman, develops a love relationship with a teenager, which leads to her falling in love. Maude does not regret any decisions she has made up to that point in her life, including her decision to end her life at the age of eighty. Arguably, Maude's decision to commit suicide may have given Harold a sense of meaning while deflating his feeble pseudo-suicide attempts.

Another form of escapism occurs when an individual retreats into pseudosenility. The most notorious illustration of this gambit occurred when a noted Mafioso attempted this in court. On a more plebian plain, many seniors become intentionally forgetful or withdrawn and helpless as a means of escaping whatever they seek to escape. As a society, the United States is experiencing increased longevity. The average age at death now extends up towards eighty (men and women combined) meaning that fully one-half of the population will remain in this stage of development for fifteen years or more.

Lawrence Dugan, Ph.D.

Theoretical and Clinical-Therapeutic Implications of Eriksonian Theory

Eriksonian Theory—first and foremost—offers a theory relating to the development of "normal" persons. As formulated by Freud, psychoanalytic theory encompasses the personality development of troubled and unhappy people. This difference, for one thing, frees a clinician to treat adult emotional problems as adult personality crises in their own right—whether they have their roots in earlier stages of development, infantile self- or other-representations, infantile frustrations and/or repressed memories.

In addition, Erikson's view of personality growth dilutes whatever onus an individual or society may have placed on parental responsibility and factors in both the role society plays and the choices the person himself makes in the formation of an individual personality. Finally, by demonstrating that each phase of growth has its strengths as well as its weaknesses, Erikson's theory offers hope that a conflict not resolved at one stage of development can be resolved at a later stage or rectified by successes at later stages. The ideas he proposes, which sound so agreeable to "common sense," can be construed as revolutionary largely based on the current divisions within the state of psychoanalysis in America.

Freud's original conception of his system emphasized the scientific aspect of psychoanalysis and, as with all sciences, left it open to revision as new facts and observations accumulated. The divisions that began with Rank and continued to the point where twenty-two different schools set themselves apart from one another distilled the meaning of psychoanalytic theory so much that psychoanalysis resembled religious factions fighting over "how many angels can dance on the head of a pin."

Freud's followers felt they needed to be constantly in the position of having to defend Freud's views. Freud's system then became, in the hands of some of his followers and defenders, orthodoxy—dogma upon which all theoretical innovation, clinical observation and therapeutic practice had to be grounded. Elkind comments, "That this attitude persists is evidenced in the recent remark by a psychoanalyst that he believed psychotic patients could not be treated by psychoanalysis because 'Freud said so.' Such attitudes, in which Freud's authority rather than observation and data is the basis of deciding what is true and what is false, contributes to the disrepute in which psychoanalysis is widely held today."

This attitude—Freud's absolute authority supersedes every other consideration in determining truth and falsehood—is referred to as Neo-Scholasticism. Erikson's theory counters such thinking and promulgates the idea that Freud's discoveries did not and should not arrest the study and development of the human psyche. Erikson not only suggested modifying analytic theory, he openly promoted modifying psychotherapeutic practices. "Young people in severe trouble are not fit for the couch," he writes. "They want to face you, and they want you to face them, not as a facsimile of a parent, or wearing the mask of a professional helper, but as a kind of overall individual a young person can live with or despair of."

Ultimately, Erikson also addressed the negative effects that distorted notions of psychoanalysis have had on society at large. Psychoanalysis, he says, had contributed to a widespread fatalism—"even as we were trying to devise, with scientific determinism, a therapy for the few, we were led to promote an ethical disease among the many." It is this spirit as well as the implications in Erikson's own writings that suggest how he could be open to expanding the theory to fit with clinical and sociological observations and subject to—if not guiding—additional research.

As psychoanalysis heads into the future with all conceivable new sociological observations, new clinical data and new research, psychoanalytic theory must be sufficiently comprehensive to embrace the diversity that such data present. At the same time, theory cannot be so open as to lose the potential to generate "testable" hypotheses—thereby becoming meaningless.

Meaningful psychoanalytic theory will serve to foment and focus research efforts in other disciplines including Medicine, Neurology, Clinical Psychology and Sociology in the service of advancing all scientific thinking. Neoscholastic thinking will not.

CHAPTER 12

Analyzing Psychoanalysis: Now and Beyond

I ronically medical science today finds itself in a position very much like its position a century ago when Freud first proposed his breakthrough thinking. Then the occurrence of disorders with no medical explanation (i.e., hysteria) had mushroomed; today the prevalence of psychosomatic disorders, such as Irritable Bowel Syndrome, Fibromyalgia, mysterious conditions associated with back pain and tension myositis syndrome (TMS)—a painful disorder affecting millions, has reached epidemic proportions, increasing tenfold over the course of the past twenty years. Now, as was true then, medical science progresses geometrically; yet, statistics indicate that the average person requires more medical treatment.

The status of psychoanalysis is far less clear. On the one hand, during the time period 1985–2005, increasing numbers of applicants sought admission to psychoanalytic institutes. By the year 2000 there were thirty-five training institutes for psychoanalysis in the United States and more than three thousand graduated psychoanalysts practicing in the United States. Such a statistic provides evidence that, like Freud's followers, professionals today carry "with them the founding fathers immense belief in psychoanalysis as a treatment modality." The fact that the majority (seventy to eighty percent) of incoming students are trained in arenas other than medicine might be considered potentially beneficial, as they bring to psychoanalysis differing backgrounds and experiences that will contribute to furthering psychoanalytic openness.

On the other hand, psychoanalysis has become relegated by many to an arcane intellectual exercise serving the wealthy, whose desire for self-scrutiny reflects fundamental narcissism. Thomas Svolos in his article "The Past and Future of Psychoanalysis in Psychiatry" also attributes the depreciation of psychoanalytic thinking in scientific circles to the conflict between psychoanalysis versus what Svolos refers to as Freudianism. Therefore, achieving an audience beyond those in training institutes and academia constitutes a significant challenge.

Svolos comments: "It has been in France and Western Europe where psychoanalysis has suffered the least from these assaults. I would assert that the reason for this is that practice in these countries has been the psychoanalysis associated with work of Jacques Lacan. Lacanian psychoanalysis is best understood as drawing its strengths from the logic of psychoanalysis itself—and a development of psychoanalysis as an autonomous discourse—to the exclusion of Freudianism. In fact, in Seminar 17, *L'envers de la psychanalyse*, Lacan sets his project as identifying the desire of Freud and elaborating a psychoanalysis without that desire."

"If there is to be a return to psychoanalysis in America, it will happen only in as much as this psychoanalysis stays true to psychoanalysis to the exclusion of Freudianism . . ." The dilemma with Freudianism—as Svolos points out—stems from the core premise of Freudianism that the analyst already has the answer regarding what is troubling the patient, i.e., unresolved oedipal feelings and fantasies. Such an attitude is tantamount to a physician deciding that every patient walking into his office requires a major tranquilizer—even before taking a history or analyzing diagnostic tests.

Svolos addresses other concerns in predicting a dim future for American psychoanalysis:

I will indicate here what I believe to be one of the most significant components of such a practice (psychoanalysis), namely, a refusal of the analyst to occupy a certain preestablished position in his work with patients. Standard advice in some schools of psychoanalysis is for the analyst to take a position of paternal authority, i.e., the analyst must take on the role of the father, regress the patient in the therapy to the time of the Oedipus complex, and maneuver the patient through it . . . or take on the role of the mother to give the patient a certain attachment security that he was unable to find in his childhood. In contrast to this advice, I believe that the analyst must take the position of nothing. . . . The analyst must allow the patient to make of the analyst what he will. . . . With this technique, the unconscious of the analysand will reveal itself, instead of the theories of the analyst. . . . This refusal of mastery and of knowledge on the part of the analyst is much harder to achieve than most realize."

With regard to the practice of interpreting every act and thought of the patient as relating first and foremost to the analyst, Svolos recognizes this practice as too automated and—in some cases—meaningless: "The therapist pays attention to ways in which the patient projects previous object relationships into the present interactions with the therapist. Most therapies incorporate aspects of object relations theory when they conceptualize the therapy as helping the patient resolve the pathological qualities of past relationships through the corrective emotional experience of the real relationship between therapist and patient."

Svolos identifies key questions he feels psychoanalysis needs to address:

"Can psychoanalysis develop consistency without creating orthodoxy and mental adherence to a rigid closed system?"

"Can those adhering to a psychoanalytic orientation ignore inconsequential differences in theory and practice and emphasize integrating common findings among practitioners?"

"How can psychoanalytic thinking direct research that will best integrate with research findings in clinical medicine, psychology and sociology?"

71

Svolos stands as uniquely qualified to comment regarding classical Freudian psychoanalysis since his own psychoanalysis involved the standard Freudian approach—and was notably effective. Recognizing that his personal experiences applied to him and may not necessarily apply to others represents a psychoanalytic thinking that strips both egoism and slavish adherence to orthodoxy from the psychoanalytic process as articulated below (Chapters Thirteen and Fourteen)

Above and beyond Svolos' critiques, proponents for broadening the conception of psychoanalysis point to the fact that psychoanalysis—operating as Freudianism—has long operated in a vacuum, ignoring issues that psychoanalysis can address in a healthy scientific manner. The additional issues cited below represent a sampling of important questions relating to psychoanalysis and psychoanalytic thinking in the twenty-first century and beyond—many more could be added. Each topic discussed could itself serve as the subject of several books. Discussing each here is a starting point for extending psychoanalytic thinking into realms previously unexplored.

"Hard Science" and Psychoanalysis

In the future all medical practitioners will increasingly confront the issue of psychosomatic illnesses. This implies that psychoanalysis has significant potential—as it did in 1900—to contribute to medical science and medical practice. However, in order to contribute significantly, psychoanalysis must move beyond Freudianism and cloistered thinking to a more scientific and open-minded analysis to communicate with other medical professionals. At the same time, other medical sciences, in particular those that address conditions where psychosomatic illnesses abound, must open to psychoanalytic thinking as a primary cause of disorder. Antipathy and territorial debates serve neither the patient nor scientific progress.

Doctor John Sarno in the Introduction to his book *The Divided Mind: The Epidemic of Mindbody Disorders*, states

"I came upon psychosomatic medicine well along in my profession when I began to see large numbers of people suffering from those common but sometimes mysterious conditions associated with bodily pain, primarily of the low back, neck, trunk, and limbs. I did not know these disorders were psychosomatic. I had not trained in psychiatry or psychology, and it was only through direct daily contact with the suffering of my patients that I came to recognize the true nature of their distress and could then begin to administer effective treatment. . . . I've published three books to describe our work, our discoveries and our successes. Those dealt largely with what I called the tension myositis syndrome (TMS), a painful disorder affecting millions. *The Divided Mind* will deal with the full range of psychosomatic disorders, a far broader and more important subject. Psychosomatic disorders fall into two categories:

Disorders directly induced by Unconscious emotions, such as the pain problems (TMS) and common gastrointestinal conditions including reflux, ulcers, irritable bowel syndrome (IBS), skin disorders and allergies.

Diseases in which Unconscious emotions may play a role in causation but are not the only factor. No one, as far as I know, who is currently studying these disorders includes unconscious emotions as potential risk factors. To my mind, this borders on criminal neglect."

Sarno proceeds to state that the incidence of chronic back pain, asthma, ulcers, Irritable Bowel Syndrome and several forms of arthritis has multiplied tenfold. He cites findings from the American Dermatology Association that seventy percent of all manifestations of skin disorders have a primary emotional factor contributing to the illness. Sarno—having been trained in the "hard sciences" and having worked twenty years as a traditional practitioner—became aware that forces were at work in his patients that transcended the traditional medical approach he had learned.

How did a man indoctrinated into the "hard sciences" arrive at the position he did? He had no psychiatric training except the mandatory six-week rotation expected of medical students and interns. He addresses that question in his Preface by stating that he became aware of how unconscious feelings and thoughts that a patient has blocked contributed to the patient's symptoms "through direct daily contact with the suffering of my patients"—in short, by observing (the foundation of all science) firsthand what needed to be observed and by listening to the patient. After twenty years as a traditional practitioner, he realized that he could serve his patients better by addressing the genuine cause of their symptoms.

Sarno's intent in writing *The Divided Mind* was "to draw attention to the blinkered attitudes of too many practitioners of contemporary medicine who fail not only to acknowledge the existence of psychosomatic disorders and (sic) who actually contribute to the spread [of psychosomatic disorders) by their failure to do so." Sarno clearly identifies the need for psychoanalysis to extend beyond the boundaries of one on one clinical treatment to impact training of physicians. Such a stance also implies that psychologists and others with psychoanalytic training will need to inform themselves regarding medical symptoms and treatments

Dr. Sarno's open-mindedness balancing "hard science" and psychoanalysis contrasts with that of another gastroenterologist: John W presented as a twenty-three-year-old young man with a thirteen-year history of ulcerative colitis. Youngest of six sons, none of whom were married (a statistical anomaly at best and certainly suggesting of some psychodynamic contribution), John entered treatment despite the objections of his mother. After six months treatment in a traditional analytic venue, John went to his gastroenterologist for his biannual checkup.

Two days later, the doctor's office called to tell him to return to have his studies redone. Three days after that, the office called to tell him to return once again. When John asked why, the nurse informed him, ". . . there's something wrong, your x-rays show no ulcers."

John met with the doctor, who congratulated him on complying with his medical regime so well (hitherto, an issue). When John informed him (as he had informed me months earlier) that he had stopped taking the medication, his doctor told him that that was impossible.

Consider the facts of the situation. The x-rays demonstrated dramatic change. The patient honestly reported having ceased taking his medication. The physician—allegedly a man of science—tells him that that cannot be. That is not scientific. Scientific thinking—from every perspective—needs to prevail, especially with regard to psychosomatic illnesses.

Consider the opposite issue—an illness believed considered to be psychologically caused having an organic etiology—as offered by Dr. V. J. Ramachandran in his work *Phantoms in the Brain*. He tells the story of Dr. Bill Marshall, a young resident physician in Australia, who looked at a stained section of ulcers under a microscope and noticed that it was teeming with Helicobacter pylori—a common bacterium found in a certain proportion of healthy individuals. Since he regularly observed these bacteria in ulcers, he started wondering if they actually caused ulcers. When he mentioned this idea to his professors, he was told, "No way! That can't be true. We all know ulcers are caused by stress. What you are seeing is just a secondary infection of an ulcer that was already in place."

"But Dr. Marshall was not dissuaded and proceeded to challenge the conventional wisdom. First he carried out an epidemiological study. . . . But this finding did not convince his colleagues . . . so—out of sheer desperation—Marshall swallowed a culture of the bacteria and a few weeks later did an endoscopy on himself to demonstrate that his gastrointestinal tract was studded with ulcers."

Ramachandran proceeds to relate that subsequent research demonstrated that patients "who were given standard treatment in combination with a bactericide recovered at a higher rate—and had fewer relapses—than did a control group given acid blocking agents alone."

In this instance, scientific thinking—and attendant evidence—remained prisoner to a group of individuals' (the professors on the faculty) preexisting belief. Like Dr. Sarno, Dr. Marshall—by observing (the foundation of all science) firsthand what needed to be observed—and not being dissuaded by "conventional wisdom" or senior professors—advanced science. To hold that ulcerative colitis can have either one of two distinct causative agents or—in many cases, both, or perhaps even a third—appears more scientific than denying the contribution of either factor by itself or in combination with other factors.

Dr. V. J. Ramachandran has been identified as one of the one hundred most important scientists to watch in the twenty-first century. He has done seminal work on the nature of—and treatment for— phantom limb pain. His willingness to conduct unusual research and to extend the barriers of neurology into hitherto unexplored areas and his convictions regarding science coupled with his willingness to extrapolate beyond the limited findings to the broader issue of understanding the mind provides not only neurology, but psychoanalysis significant value.

In his Preface to *Phantoms in the Brain* Ramachandran offers all scientists incredible food for thought.

A tension exists in neurology and, I add, medicine and psychoanalysis between those who believe that the most valuable lessons about the brain can be learned from statistical analyses involving large numbers of patients and those who believe that doing the right kind of experiments on the right patients—even a single patient—can yield much more useful information. This is really a silly debate since its resolution is obvious: It's a good idea to begin with experiments on single cases and then to confirm the findings through the studies of additional patients. By way of analogy, imagine that I cart a pig into your living room and tell you that it can walk. You might say 'Oh, really? Show me!' I then wave my wand and the pig starts walking. You might respond 'My God! That's amazing!' You are not likely to say 'Ah, but that's just one pig. Show me a few more and I might believe you.' Yet this is precisely the attitude of many people in my field.

Ramachandran provides other evidence regarding the study of the individual. "More was learned about memory from a few days studying a patient called H. M. that was gleaned from previous decades of research averaging data on many subjects."

Additionally, in the interest of science and scientific thinking, Ramachandran addresses the pejorative connotation assigned to the word speculation: "Describing someone's ideas as 'mere speculation' is often considered insulting. This is unfortunate. As the English biologist Perer Medawar has noted, 'An imaginative conception of what might be true is the starting point of all great discoveries in science.'"

Psychoanalysis represents the *sine qua non* of opportunities to employ single case studies to expand the science of the mind. Addressing unresolved unconscious issues of a patient demands that the analyst speculate regarding etiology and interpretation. What is left is to document findings and communicate those findings in a forum that will benefit other practitioners.

The two examples cited above that focused on ulcers strive to argue not for one position or another, but for scientific objectivity consistent with that proposed by Ramachandran. The thinking involved regarding the need for scientific discipline applies equally to Anxiety Disorders, Depression and Character Disorders (including Borderline Personality) and even neurological disorders, i.e., considering psychoanalysis as treatment in combination with—or instead of—medications. Direct clinical experience (my own and others) indicates that greater than seventy percent of patients who sought to eliminate medications achieved that goal, using a well defined protocol—tapering off medications as they resolved unconscious issues to overcome depression and anxiety permanently. Such sampling is obviously biased, yet even standard statistical analysis would reveal such results to be highly improbable unless the treatment had value.

No contradiction between "hard science" and psychoanalysis exists—nor can it—so long as the emphasis remains on the results for a patient. Truth—though exceedingly complex at times—stands as unitary and, hopefully, uniting. Science embraces both knowledge and belief. The saying "For those who believe, no proof is necessary. For those who disbelieve, no amount of proof is sufficient" offers all scientists opportunities to challenge their own belief system, i.e., to try to prove their beliefs untrue. How open can they be to truth especially when that truth challenges the very core of what they have learned?

Psychoanalysis and Being Christian

In 1950 the World Council of Churches condemned psychoanalysis as "a tool of the devil"—a position predicated on several factors, not the least of which involved a lack of genuine understanding of psychoanalysis. Today differences in attitude towards psychoanalysis among Christian churches vary significantly. Extremely conservative churches maintain a position that, if not openly condemning of psychoanalysis, does not support it; others see psychoanalysis as irrelevant; still others deem it in the same vein as they might deem other medical treatment.

For its part, throughout history psychoanalysis has ignored Christian beliefs as irrelevant to psychoanalysis (or, regrettably, interpreted Christian beliefs as a variety of defense mechanisms, i.e., Denial, Escapism, etc.). Neither attitude reflects healthy scientific thinking. From a psychoanalytic perspective religious belief is as relevant to psychoanalytic scrutiny as are other shapers of thoughts and feelings, i.e., early abandonment, physical abuse, etc. Just as there can be no contradiction between "hard science" and psychoanalysis, the premise regarding Christianity and psychoanalysis reflects the counsel, "Render to Caesar the things that are Caesar's and to God the things that are God's."

For the purposes of this discussion, an individual is Christian if he meets the following criteria:

Does this person state that he has a personal relationship with Jesus Christ, who is the Son of God and died on the Cross to redeem the sins of all mankind?

Does this person attempt to live his life in accordance with Jesus' words? From among several Scriptural references Luke 10:25-30 stands out: "And behold, a lawyer stood up to put him to the test, saying, 'Teacher, what shall I do to inherit eternal life?' He said to him, 'What is written in the law? How do you read?' And the lawyer answered, "You shall love the Lord your God with all your heart, and with all your soul, and with all your strength, and with your entire mind; and your neighbor as yourself.' And Jesus said to him, 'You have answered right; do this, and you will live.'"

Jesus, however, spells out precisely what he means by loving your neighbor in Matthew 25:31-40. "Then the King will tell those on his right hand, 'Come, blessed of my Father, inherit the kingdom prepared for you from the foundation of the world for I was hungry, and you gave me food to eat; I was thirsty, and you gave me drink; I was a stranger, and you took me in; naked, and you clothed me; I was sick, and you visited me; I was in prison, and you came to me.' Then the righteous will answer him, saying, 'Lord, when did we see you hungry, and feed you; or thirsty, and give you a drink? When did we see you as a stranger, and take you in; or naked, and clothe you? When did we see you sick, or in prison, and come to you?' The King will answer them, 'Most assuredly I tell you, inasmuch as you did it to one of the least of these my brothers, you did it to me.'"

This "reptilian brain" (black-white thinking) focus on what it means to be Christian addresses the core of what the majority of Christian churches agree to and avoids theological or doctrinal differences based on history and or miscommunications from the founder of a denomination.

In a parallel manner, applying a litmus test to determine an individual's psychoanalytic orientation involves asking the following questions:

- Does this person believe that repressed unconscious thoughts and feelings can cause physical illness and untold disruptions in human beings?
- Does he believe that bringing these issues to consciousness to resolve them can—in and of itself (no other treatment)—be healing to the individual?

The person who answers "yes" to both sets of questions will differ significantly from the person who responds "no" to both and from those who respond with one "yes" and one "no."

Based on the above definition of being a Christian, characteristics relevant to psychoanalysis emerge. First, being Christian demands true humility. Christians daily recognize an infinite, all powerful God—the Creator of billions of galaxies and all of the nature we experience every day and the Designer of the evolutionary system and biological system that is summarized at the beginning of this book.

God is The Completely Other. Grasping this concept requires thinking in metaphors: Think about a gnat trying to understand a human being. Given our knowledge of gnats, such a concept lies beyond conception. Yet we are much further removed from God than a gnat is from us. Human beings will never understand—or know—God. To make that truth the central theme of one's mind demands humility.

At the same time, that humility has embedded within it healthy self-love. In what emerges as the ultimate mental paradox faced by human beings, Christians assert that this all-powerful God, who existed before Time and who has absolutely no need of anything from humans, loves and accepts the individual—would we love and accept a gnat?—so much so that he took on human form to feel the pain of being tortured and crucified and died as a human so we could eventually share in His glory in a world beyond this one.

If attempting to conceive of God is impossible, grasping the meaning of the core Christian belief regarding Jesus is unimaginable. Think in terms of this metaphor. Imagine yourself richer than Bill Gates or Warren Buffet—possessing every material benefit you can imagine. Now, imagine you take yourself to the most squalid corner of the world with disease and filth so you can work among those people; that you are abused and rejected by them; and then, after having been tortured, you are nailed to a cross. Even knowing that by doing that, you save thousands of lives, could you do it?

To accept that God in the person of Jesus Christ did exactly that reinforces the humility a Christian has and adds to that humility both incredible love for God and—based on being loved by an infinite and awesome God—genuine self-love. That healthy self-love demands that a Christian love others in the same manner. Psychologically this signifies both an intellectual-imaginative capacity and an emotional commitment that sets apart those who accept that challenge.

Explaining that concept—from a purely psychoanalytic perspective—indicates that the individual who achieves that state creates a completely different inner self-representation, a self-representation that differs from all other self-representations since that representation is not just me as a psychic entity, but me-with-God (Jesus Christ/the-Holy Spirit)-in-me. Even striving to achieve such high standards on one's own merit becomes impossible. An individual's recognition that he cannot do it alone psychologically transforms the person at the level of the reptilian brain and thus becomes a primal motivating force.

Freud himself recognized that the concept of perfection fit within human experience when he alluded to the ego ideal—"an image of the perfect self towards which the ego should aspire." The inner representation identified here exceeds the ego-ideal proposed by Freud. The me-with-God-in-me self-representation exists at the reptilian/mammalian brain level, not just in the neocortex. Far beyond intellectually knowing God or believing in God, this new self-representation results from experiencing

81

God. Dr. V. J. Ramachandran argues that "human beings have actually evolved specialized neural circuitry for the sole purpose of mediating religious experiences." He relates how Dr. Michael Persinger in his work with a transcranial magnetic stimulator, stimulated his temporal lobes, including the underlying limbic system (reptilian brain), and for the first time in his life experienced God!

In using the particular phrase "experienced God," Persinger clarified what is—theologically and psychoanalytically—extremely significant. Experiencing God represents a quantum leap difference from believing in God, knowing of God or knowing God. No metaphor will ever do justice to elucidating the difference between knowing—an intellectual, neocortical function—and experiencing—a primal survival-pleasure function. Consider the following metaphor.

For two or three minutes I describe to you a warm, fresh-from-the-oven, chocolate chip cookie. I speak of how warm and moist that cookie is. I mention the semisweet chocolate bits embedded in the brown-sugar cookie and the aroma in the kitchen. I employ every enticing word and sensory experience I can conceive. No matter what words I use or how well I describe, will any of that match your experience of actually biting into the cookie and experiencing that cookie and all those sensations for yourself? Until you taste (experience) that cookie, it is mere theory. The difference between experiencing the cookie and experiencing God lies in the fact that you likely have had prior experience with a fresh-from-the-oven chocolate chip cookie that you can relate to and draw from your memory.

Psychoanalysis addresses psychological issues. The human conception of God—our inner representation of God—develops as do other inner representations. It may be that for some, religion represents escapism or denial. Jonestown and Waco manifest evil and psychopathology parading as religion. For others unresolved unconscious issues can preclude a full emotional commitment to and belief in God—especially if those issues have been repressed and represent behavior that the individual sees as contrary to God or being accepted by God. This is a legitimate domain of psychoanalysis. To pretend that God or inner representations of God do not achieve the stature of relevance in psychoanalysis is unscientific.

CHAPTER 13

The Science of Psychoanalysis:
The Process

Sixty years ago Dr. Robert Lindner—in his classic text, *The Fifty Minute Hour*, described the psychoanalytic therapeutic process as "one of the strangest of all occupations." I dare not disagree. To peek inside the soul of a human being, continually facing the paradox of remaining impartial while empathically caring, and to let another person present the contents of his or her soul in his or her own inimical fashion presents the most challenging—and fascinating—enterprise I can conceive.

And the most gratifying.

As stated in the Preface to this book, psychoanalysis is best identified as a process in which two persons, one with comprehensive specialized knowledge about human beings, interact in a free and unstructured manner for the benefit of the one of them identified as patient. The process seems simple. The patient speaks; the analyst listens. The seeming simplicity masks the complexity.

Psychoanalysis stands out from general psychotherapy, and permutations of treatment evolved starting in the 1960's. Microscopic pieces of theory were isolated and established as a comprehensive approach to treatment. Reactions against the rigidity of Freudianism led to schools that ignored developmental issues and helping a patient understand the source of his problem, emphasizing instead that all would be healed if the patient had the opportunity to vent. Other schools emphasized the need for the patient to obtain emotional support from the therapist. "Holding" became a byword of the 1960's and 1970's. Psychoanalytic psychotherapy became passé—representing another reaction against Freudianism. Research findings indicating that psychotherapy is ineffective likely resulted from not having well-defined standards by which to define both quality of training and grounding in knowledge.

In order to be effective, psychotherapy needs to consist of more than an opportunity for the patient to vent and/or deriving emotional support from a therapist. Both elements need to be embedded in a much deeper context—a developmental-psychoanalytic context—if the results of therapy are to endure and an individual achieve full mental health. Psychoanalysis (psychoanalytic psychotherapy) stands as different by dint of the knowledge the therapist must bring to the interaction with the patient. His knowledge of defense mechanisms and his awareness of developmental (Eriksonian) Theory, along with issues to look and listen for, constitute one pillar of his knowledge. His ability to analyze the meaning behind the patient's words and actions constitutes yet another.

Psychoanalysis operates with premises regarding a patient seeking help. Seeking help does not come readily to human beings. The level of pain must reach a certain point before the individual seeks help—especially if the person defines what lies behind seeking help as a flaw in character. The patient will (unconsciously) test the therapist. He or she will enter thinking—or wishing—the problem is the husband or the spouse or the job. He enters the world of therapy uncertain, often convincing himself that he just seeks emotional support. He starts by sharing with the therapist one piece of a jigsaw puzzle trusting (and hoping) that the analyst will see the entire picture, look at that single piece and see the whole puzzle and—more importantly—detect what lies behind the puzzle.

Years ago, Sir William Osler, founder of Johns Hopkins Medical School and considered by many to be the founder of modern medicine, uttered his famous mandate: "Listen to the patient. He is telling you the diagnosis." This axiom remains as true, if not truer, today as it did back in Sir Osler's time. While true for all medicine, it must be considered particularly true for those serving patients that seek treatment for emotional distress. The starting point for the psychoanalytic process is: Listen to the patient. Any other course of action constitutes a travesty to the highest degree.

In *The Fifty Minute Hour*, Lindner also suggests the simplicity of the psychoanalytic process, addressing the issue in this manner: "Around psychoanalysis there has been built a fence of mystery and something resembling awe . . .this cabalistic climate which today surrounds the practice of psychoanalysis has had some weird and, I think, harmful effects. . . . Not the least among them has been the conversion of the psychoanalyst . . . to a kind of devil's disciple who works with means arcane and mystic to secure the transformations of character or personality he desires. Nothing could be further from the truth."

If the psychoanalytic process does border on the mystical, the simplicity of the process renders it so. The simplicity involves a single rule: Listen to the patient. Indeed, to be as Lindner invites analysts to be, "artists at understanding," can we do other than listen to the patient? Our primary task is to take what the patient gives us, analyze and interpret, then reflect it back in such a manner that he can fully integrate it into the very fabric of his being. This process of analyzing, interpreting, and reflecting and having the patient internalize the meaning and the accuracy of the reflection thus allows the patient to overcome the past and transform the future.

However, the crux of analysis is to continually search for the meanings behind every utterance the patient makes. It is the analyst's ability to detect the meaning below the surface— defenses and resistances to more primal thoughts—that renders psychoanalysis unique and powerful.

Listening to the patient means letting the patient talk in a free-flowing venue; it means listening to what is not being said, as well as what is being said. In more interactive psychoanalytic psychotherapy, questioning in an open-ended way—or making a well-thought reflective comment—prompts patients to reveal what they do not consciously seek to reveal. Years ago one of my patients referred to "looking for Mr. Goodbar," opening up the avenue to examining her lifelong battle with suicidal feelings and, eventually, the source of those feelings. More recently a patient referred to herself as a cowgirl. Knowing she had never left city limits, her analyst simply said, "Tell me more," evoking a deeper meaning of her statement. Even saying "I don't understand" will lead a patient to show more pieces of the puzzle.

What is it that a patient gives us? What are the data from which we start to understand our fellow human? Simply, a patient reveals the unrefined contents of a mind—the flotsam and jetsam from hidden corners, which constitute the evidence of psychic scars and long forgotten feelings. It is the analyst's job, as artists with knowledge of "man and all his aspects," to take the "glimpses of the soul" that a patient gives and work to determine their meaning.

Like all science, psychoanalysis operates not only with rules and processes, but also on the basis of proof. Lindner presents five cases demonstrating the scientific connections between adult behavior and early childhood experiences. Earlier, in analyzing infant experiences, I referred to how "discrete units of memory (with their attendant feelings) combine to form images. The image of "mother," for example, can include the "good breast" the "bad breast," warmth, distance, soothing voice, different touches and thousands of events and sensations impossible to imagine. With constantly repeated experience the infant will form a smaller number of images, some of which may still conflict with one another. If the "mothering" is inconsistent or consistently cold or consistently painful, the infant will create an image of the world that defies our ability to define or understand—an image that will bring with it terror, rage, helplessness, self-loathing and more. The image of "self" created will be that of worthlessness, revenge seeking and death seeking."

The patient Matt V presented with a deep and abiding hatred of women and fantasies of doing violence to them (never acted on). After Matt had been in therapy for four years, his sister, ten years older, shared with him events she had witnessed when he was still in the crib. Matt confronted his mother who admitted that being alone on occasions and not having adequately prepared for motherhood, she recalled five "episodes"—four where she stuck him with a pin, the fifth where she pinched his penis. Within six weeks following this revelation, Matt experienced significant changes in his behavior and feelings.

As a science, psychoanalysis requires evidence of results. Not all patients have the fortune of being able to verify their fears, fantasies or memories. Verification is less significant than the alleviation of symptoms. John, the young man with ulcers cited above, expressed strong feelings regarding his mother's intrusiveness that led to him not needing his medication. The proof may not be as satisfactory as analyst or patient would prefer. Replicability in psychoanalysis focuses on ever-shifting data and the unreliable human mind. Distinguishing between reality and fear and fantasy does not always come easily.

The results will validate the interpretations.

One last reflection. Some psychoanalysts have suggested that its concepts and theories parallel those found in the humanities rather than those proper to the physical and biological/medical sciences. Paul Ricoeur, for example, argued that psychoanalysis can be considered a type of textual interpretation or hermeneutics. He contends that analysis more resembles cultural critics and literary scholars—spending time interpreting the nuances of language. Such an attitude reveals a lack of thinking and scientific analysis. Psychoanalytic interpretation does not focus on nuances of language but rather on the emotional meaning and historical connections to that language, as well as on what the patient does not say. Psychoanalytic interpretation requires significant work and an attitude (See the following chapter—*The Art of Psychoanalysis—The Analyst.*) that goes far beyond a trivial understanding of listen to the patient.

CHAPTER 14

The Art of Psychoanalysis: The Analyst

Years ago, a patient leaving a session stopped after she had opened the door and turned to look at me. "All my years growing up I never understood what people meant when they referred to a father's love. Now I do."

The art of psychotherapy lies in the heart, soul and mind of the analyst. Whatever powers the analyst possesses lie grounded not in any technical knowledge or interpretive ability, but rather in the genuine caring of the therapist and in his being as open to the patient as he is in the here and now. As analysts, we must be caring and open to the patient. Earlier I referred to the power and meaning of experience. Our experiences, as well as our interpretation of our experiences, create and shape our representations to a far greater degree than any book or testimonial.

So it is with our patients. Their experience of the therapist allows the process of psychoanalysis to proceed. I have come to the conclusion that those of us who thus engage ourselves in the practice of analytic psychotherapy are born to it. Training is required, but that training must take place on a template, a mind and heart endowed from birth with that unique disposition to seek the ultimate truth—not for one's own benefit, but for the benefit of another human being. To that disposition must be added a true humility since in this endeavor to "secure the transformation of personality" and become "artists at understanding" the therapist must commit to that previously cited rule: Listen to the patient.

Lawrence Dugan, Ph.D.

Fifty-five years ago, in his foreword to *The Fifty Minute Hour*, Lindner addressed this issue thus: "As a matter of fact, the only medium employed by the analyst is the commonest instrument of all—his own human self, utilized to the fullest in an effort to understand its fellows."

He goes on to state:

A psychoanalyst is, therefore, nothing more than an artist at understanding, the product of an intensive course of study and training which has—if it has been success-ful—rendered him unusually sensitive to his fellow men. And it is this sensitivity—in short, the analyst's own per-son—which is the single instrument, the only tool with which he performs. Only on himself and on nothing else does he depend.

The common element in all the tales that follow is the self of the analyst. Each story, while it tells of a specific "case," deals finally with the deployment of that self in the therapeutic enterprise, the adventures that befell it and the effects exerted upon it by the actors and situations described. Because the self in question is my own, and my intention far from confessional or biographical, I have exercised a cer-tain degree of discretion; but the portrait I have drawn is on the whole a quite honest one and delineates, to the best of my ability, the personality of the agent of therapy involved. That this agent is a mere human, just another person with his own hopes and fears, goals and anxieties, prejudices and pretensions, weaknesses and strengths, is really the heart of the matter.

What emerges from Lindner's description of his methodol-ogy is his commitment to enter into the mind of the patient in order to form that therapeutic alliance that will be healing. What emerges with equal strength in his writing is his recognition of the common human nature we share. "We are all responsible, defiled, and unhappy. We have stolen with the burglar whose

90

face we do not know, murdered with the parricide that we read about in the newspapers, raped with the lewd, cursed with the blasphemous." This empathic identification constitutes the essence of psychoanalysis and implies that the psychoanalyst cannot see himself as "the expert" to whom someone comes seeking "the right answers." He will better see himself as equal with his patients, a person who does possess specialized knowledge and more than anything strives to understand.

Psychoanalysis demands that the analyst subrogate his ego and ideas to a greater cause—the well-being of the patient—and in that sense become a willing student of the patient. The psychoanalyst must cleanse from his soul whatever detritus interferes with listening to the patient—including the detritus of his or her own soul and biases—so as not to defeat psychoanalysis and thus the patient.

In addition, psychoanalysis requires that the analyst achieve the emotional power of a parent—thought not power in the manner of classical Freudianism—in order for the patient to attach to the therapist. Even though the patient is not an infant or child, he lives with unresolved issues and needs to attach and identify with the therapist in order to achieve genuine enduring change. The analyst must adopt in every manner the role of a healthy parent—being genuine and open and listening and setting the patient's needs as primary—rather than adhering to a slavish preconceived notion of the root cause and operating in a power mode that more meets the analyst's needs than the patient's needs.

For example, from a psychoanalytic perspective, letting it pass when a patient makes the statement to the analyst, "You're right" constitutes a therapeutic error. Reflecting to the patient that a healthier response—one that empowers him and renders him equal to the analyst—is "I agree." For both the analyst and the patient, 'being right" constitutes a trap in the form of an ego trip.

Research conducted on psychotherapy provides valuable lessons and reflections. Robert Lang's classic definitive text,

Lawrence Dugan, Ph.D.

Psychoanalytic Psychotherapy, gives what I consider to be a crucial observation regarding the process of psychoanalysis: When a patient is not making progress, ninety percent of the time the therapist will assert that it is the patient's resistances, whereas actual studies reveal that ninety percent of the time it is therapist error or blockage causing the stalemate in therapeutic progress.

Lang's observations teach us a critical point. The process of analysis as practiced by the analyst demands more critical self-evaluation than any other conceivable process. A surgeon needs to know his limits, but will not fear that he will mistake one organ for another. A physician can rely on lab tests and x-rays to insure his diagnosis. Psychoanalysis remains the career where the doctor is the instrument; and, as such, the process of psychoanalysis is more inextricably intertwined with the soul of the practitioner than conceivable in any other endeavor.

Not everyone agrees. Dr. Lloyd Siegel—in his Introduction to *The Fifty Minute Hour*—states: "Lindner's achievement is one of humanity and daring and spirit. . . . He obviously saw the common strand of humanity that runs through every man and undertook to apply his very generous and empathic nature to the alleviation of psychic anguish without prejudice." Siegel intended these comments to be criticism, openly stating that Lindner was unscientific and the patients would today be treated with behavior modification and drugs.

More the tragedy.

Lindner did deviate from the Freudianism of the time. First and foremost, he worked with patients (two sociopaths, one a character disorder, one severely depressed and the last highly delusional) that Freud himself would have declared untreatable. I offer the proposition that Lindner's work demonstrated the power of psychoanalysis and that Lindner chose the better path. In reflecting on Siegel's comments, ask: If the role of the analyst is not to apply a generous and giving nature to alleviate suffering, what is it? If the analyst is not to seek achievements of humanity and daring and spirit, what is he to seek?

Scientific thinking by its very nature focuses on the result with a patient. Psychoanalysis cannot set itself apart in this regard. Replicability leads to credibility. If analysts in three different cities treat patients with ulcerative disorders and all three become cured, does that prove that some forms of ulcerative disorders are purely psychological in origin? How many pigs have to walk before . . . ?

Closing Thoughts

The human mind stands among the last great frontiers for science. Psychoanalysis needs to decide whether to stand and work with other neurosciences to address the multiple issues they share—particularly the impact of emotional development on psychosomatic illnesses and other mental functioning—or to retreat to a path of Freudianism and continued fractionalization and end up atop a dung heap of archaic knowledge. Achieving the former demands that psychoanalysis adjust its current course; the latter will result from doing nothing to change.

Issues abound. The over-sixty population will surpass fifty million by the year 2016, leading to complex social and psychological issues for the individuals, their families and society. The incidence of psychosomatic disorders will continue to rise exponentially. The incidence of Depressive Disorders and Anxiety Disorders will also continue to rise geometrically. Mental health and medical professionals need good training in order to triage and treat the thousands of patients they will confront. Psychoanalysis needs to decide whether to remain an esoteric practice, operating solely as an esoteric practice servicing an elite few, or a science and service making it possible to have well-trained, analytically oriented professionals available in every village to assist physicians in diagnosing psychosomatic disorders, as well as young people in choosing the right partner for the right reasons.

To paraphrase an ancient Jewish scholar: "If not us, who? If not now, when?"

LaVergne, TN USA
06 July 2010
188488LV00005B/1/P